One on One

The Way of a Disciple

A Nine-Week Guide to One-on-one Mentoring

Leader Guide

The Evangelical Catholic

www.evangelicalcatholic.org

Table of Contents

Introduction

Sue had a powerful experience on a weekend retreat. For the first time in her life as a Catholic she encountered Christ and felt that he was real, that he knew her by name, and that he was calling her. She desired to open her heart and put Christ at the center of her life. The Mass came alive for her as never before. She participated with enthusiasm, really wanting to pray the responses.

Sue returned home after the retreat and continued to attend Mass at her parish. She tried to find a small group or someone to whom to talk about her experience but was unable to make any connections. She continued to go to Mass. After a few weeks, though, she began to feel the fire that burned within her dwindling. She felt discouraged and doubtful about her own experience. She knew she should probably pray but had no idea how to do it.

Sue experienced what Benedict XVI terms "an encounter with an event, a person, which gives life a new horizon and a decisive direction."[1] She underwent initial interior conversion to Christ. What needs did she have after this encounter? What happened to her in the weeks that followed that experience? Jesus' observations in the Gospel of Matthew relate to this not uncommon story:

> When he [Jesus] saw the crowds, he had compassion for them, because they were harassed and helpless, like sheep without a shepherd. Then he said to his disciples, "The harvest is plentiful, but the laborers are few, therefore ask the Lord of the harvest to send out laborers into his harvest."[2]

Sue didn't know how to follow Christ so she slowed on the path and began to lose sight of Christ. She did not know how to nourish her relationship with Christ through word and sacrament. She failed to find an intense Christian community like the one at the retreat. Sue didn't know what following Christ involved or what a disciple must do to lead to life in him. Sue needed a laborer. She needed someone to intentionally befriend her and apprentice her into the Christian life.

The Church calls this necessary step in the whole process of evangelization "initiatory catechesis" and describes it in this way:

> The "moment" of catechesis is that which corresponds to the period in which conversion to Jesus Christ is formalized, and provides a basis for first adhering

---

[1] Pope Benedict XVI, Deus Caritas Est, 1, 2006.
[2] Matthew 9: 36-38

to him. Converts, by means of "a period of formation, an **apprenticeship** in the whole Christian life", are initiated into the mystery of salvation and an evangelical style of life. This means "initiating the hearers into the fullness of Christian life [emphasis added]".[3]

As an apprentice in Christian life, your discipleship partner needs this special period of time the Church describes above to receive individual care and help learning the ways of Christ. This apprenticeship makes possible the joyful evangelical life Sue tasted during initial conversion, but could not find again.

Often someone like Sue either falls back into her pre-conversion style of life, or becomes involved in church leadership too soon, not having had the opportunity to grow and mature before becoming a worker and leader. Just as Jesus saw the necessity for shepherds who could guide and care for his sheep, so the Church recognizes how crucial initiatory catechesis is,

> Initiatory catechesis is thus the necessary link between missionary activity which calls to faith and pastoral activity which continually nourishes the Christian community. This is not, therefore, an optional activity, but basic and fundamental for building up the personality of the individual disciple, as it is for the whole Christian community. Without it, missionary activity lacks continuity and is sterile, while pastoral activity lacks roots and becomes superficial and confused: any misfortune could cause the collapse of the entire building.[4]

The Church has special need now for workers to respond to the call of Jesus to "go and make disciples." The Holy Spirit has called you to labor for and with Christ so that his sheep can receive guidance and encouragement. He has given you zeal for the work of evangelization and the love and patience of the Good Shepherd who cares deeply for his sheep and wants to see them grow and flourish.

The Scriptures witness to the personal sacrifice and love that one-on-one ministry requires as well as the rewards. In his first letter to the Thessalonians St. Paul writes, "we were gentle among you, like a nurse tenderly caring for her own children. So deeply do we care for you that we are determined to share with you not only the gospel of God but also our own selves, because you have become very dear to us."[5]

Thank you for responding to the Holy Spirit's call to help his people become disciples.

[3] Congregation for the Clergy, General Directory for Catechesis, paragraph 63, United States Catholic Conference, Washington, D.C., 1997.
[4] Ibid., 64.
[5] I Thessalonians 2: 7-8

These materials are designed to support you in this great task. The following sections will explain the materials and coach you in using this guide. Your booklet is the same as your discipleship partner's except for the introduction, the italicized leader notes and the sections before the Week 1. None of these appear in the discipleship partner's booklet. Other than this the leader's guide and the discipleship partner's guide both have all the same text and questions.

Format of Weekly Sessions

Location

For the initial meeting, a coffee shop, restaurant or other public place on campus will work fine. The topics become more personal later. Meeting in a more private setting that is comfortable and inviting may then be preferable. This could allow for more disclosure and greater ease during opening and closing prayer.

Duration of Meeting Time

At the end of your initial meeting or when the person has expressed interest in meeting one-on-one with regularity, decide how long you will meet each week. We suggest meeting for at least one hour and fifteen minutes or better for one hour and a half. The sessions can be completed in an hour but not easily, and an hour allows no time for warming up with conversation.

Opening Prayer and Closing Prayer

Before praying together at the beginning of your session, spend a little time catching up. Ask simple opening questions such as: "How was your week" or "How have you been?" Do not appear hurried. Sometimes "small talk" reveals what that person really needs to discuss. Your ability to listen well, to interiorly ask the Holy Spirit for guidance, and to helpfully question your discipleship partner is extremely important.

It is also important, however, not to spend too much time in small talk, especially if your meetings are less than 1 hour and a half. The responsibility to transition to the opening prayer and the topic is on you, the leader. Asking if you can open up your time together in prayer can be a great way to transition to the material and topic for that week.

Pre-written opening and closing prayers will not be provided in the weekly sessions of this booklet. This is intentional so that mentors model and practice spontaneous and personal conversational prayer with our friend, Jesus Christ.

Modeling and inviting your discipleship partner into conversational prayer is an essential element of this apprenticeship. If you know your partner would be comfortable or up to the challenge for the third session, invite her to begin your opening prayer and then tell her that you will pray after her. When both leader and discipleship partner contribute to the opening and closing prayers, the discipleship partner has two opportunities to voice her prayer (at the beginning and end of each session) and to listen to prayer modeled. This is an important opportunity for growth for the discipleship partner. It also provides a time for you to listen carefully for the discipleship partner's concerns so you can address them at another time.

If your discipleship partner does not seem comfortable in the first session or two, invite her to open up in prayer after a few weeks of seeing you model it. It is the leader's responsibility to set the discipleship partner at ease during prayer times by giving clear directions before starting. If you are at ease, they will feel more comfortable. Below is a sample dialogue and prayer:

Leader: Jenny, would you be willing to open us up in prayer today? Are you comfortable with that?

Jenny: I haven't really done that before but sure.

Leader: That's great. Just don't worry about needing to sound eloquent. Let's start with a few seconds of silence to place ourselves in God's presence. Then as you pray, I'll pray interiorly with you. After you pray, I'll offer a prayer as well and then why don't we end with a Glory Be?

Jenny: Okay. In the name of the Father... (Pause.) God, please be with us today as we discuss...

Leader: We thank you, God, for the time we have together today... Holy Spirit, we ask you to open our hearts and minds...

Sample opening prayer:

> Lord, we pause to allow ourselves to enter into your presence. (Pause) Thank you for always being with us. We ask you to be with us in a special way right now. Holy Spirit, please guide our time together. Help us to open our hearts and minds to you and to recognize you in one another. We ask this through Jesus Christ, our Lord. Amen.

The Wheel

Beginning with Week 2, one of the headings that will appear weekly is "The Wheel." The Wheel is a tool for learning and remembering various aspects and habits of Catholic discipleship. When you see this heading you will refer back to the Wheel in Week 2 and discuss the aspect or habit that is the focus for that session. An explanation of the Wheel and the various aspects and habits of discipleship can be found in Appendix A. It is important to visit this illustration weekly, even briefly, in order to keep the big picture of discipleship in mind and to help your discipleship partner memorize it as a tool for self examination.

Scripture for Memorization

Scripture Memory can be a transformative part of a one-on-one mentoring relationship. Memorizing Scripture with your discipleship partner provides the accountability needed for such a discipline and the opportunity to share the spiritual impact the verses have on you. Hiding God's Word in your Heart and Mind: A Catholic Topical Memory System (TMS), by Rich Cleveland offers the verses that go along with the Catholic Wheel Illustration used in this guide on small cards with a case and reflection booklet. This series can be a wonderful complement to this ten-week one-on-one series. TMS includes seventy verse cards and is an effective tool for building one's knowledge and love of Scripture. It is available for purchase at www.emmausjourney.org under "Bible Study Resources."

Italicized Notes to the Leader

All notes to the leader are written in italics and are not included in the discipleship partner's booklet. These italicized notes orient the leader to the goals, approach, and theological understanding of the topic. They also alert the leader to sensitive questions and challenging directions that a conversation could take. In addition the leader notes provide tips on how to present and facilitate various exercises. For example, the leader will introduce praying with Scripture in Week 5. The italicized notes to the leader provide essential guidance for how to guide the discipleship partner through this prayer time.

Relying on these notes, the authors did not write out section introductions and transitions in order to limit text read aloud. The onus is on you, the leader, to prepare how you will transition from one section to the next, and to explain the relationship of each section to the overarching topic.

Readings and Discussion Questions

Readings draw from Scripture, Church documents, and writings of the saints. All are important. If you do not complete a session, feel free to pick up next week where you ended during the last, depending on the needs of the discipleship partner. The sessions were designed to be completed within the session without preparatory work by discipleship partner.

Many of the readings are drawn from Scripture. The Word has a special, transformative effect and is vital during initiatory catechesis. Love for God's Word is more easily caught than taught. Leaders model love of the Word of God and guide the discipleship partners to discover the joy of understanding and praying Scripture. Invite your partner to read the passages aloud. If a reading is particularly long, offer to rotate with your partner.

Good discussion is a result of good facilitation. Good facilitation requires strong listening skills, encouraging responses, and relevant follow up questions such as:

- What was that like for you?

- What else does it say?

- What does that mean?

- Why do you think that is?

Teaching moments arise, but a discipleship leader is not a teacher. The overall pedagogy of a one-on-one is the Socratic Method (questioning and exploring ideas). Your questions should help the discipleship partners explore more deeply who Christ is and what he means in their lives.

If a question elicits only a "yes" or "no" response you will want to follow up with responses such as:

- Could you say more about that?

- What was that like?

- Would you be comfortable sharing more about that?

It is your job to draw out the discipleship partner and to lead them through the discussion. At times questions are open-ended; other times more pointed. When the questions require knowledge the discipleship partners do not have, rescue them quickly with necessary information so the question does not become a guessing game.

Tips for Leaders

Who is Ready for One-on-One Mentoring?

Persons like Sue who have been sufficiently evangelized -- that is they are turned towards Christ and they desire to learn how to follow him more closely -- are ready for the apprenticeship period one-on-one mentoring provides. Usually people who are ready for discipling are open, teachable, and display a hunger to grow and know more. Often, these are the people who attend every parish and campus ministry event simply seeking to be fed spiritually. Sometimes we call these people F.A.T., people because they are faithful, available and teachable.

After an initial introductory meeting if you discern that the person is hungry for one-on-one discipling, it is usually wise to start small. Suggest meeting weekly for one month. After that you can always invite them to continue meeting to complete the material for all nine weeks. This provides both of you with a comfortable exit if the one-on-one mentoring relationship isn't working. Most often the mentoring relationship will go well and you will continue meeting.

Asking Someone to Meet One-on-One

If your campus ministry or parish is launching a Lenten Discipleship Program or a Peer Mentoring Program in which people sign up to be paired with a leader for spiritual mentoring, no personal invitation to one-on-one mentoring is usually necessary. Personal invitation can help launch these programs when sign up is low. Often men will not sign up for such programs and must be invited. Many campus ministers find that men respond well to the invitation from other male students or priests serving the ministry.

If the discipleship partner has signed up, begin with "Meeting and Setting Goals" to get acquainted and set goals and expectations. If you already know the student or parishioner from his/her involvement or through friendship, you will want to begin with "Week 1: Important Moments in the Process of Faith and Conversion."

Without a sign-up style program, inviting a person to meet for one-on-one mentoring can be intimidating, especially if a culture of spiritual apprenticeship has not already been established at a campus ministry or parish. The following is a sample dialogue of how to approach this for two students or parishioners.

One on One

The Way of a Disciple

Leader: How are things going, Sue?

Sue: Really well…(small talk)

Leader: Great. Hey, I was wondering what you think of this. Would you be interested in meeting with me a few times to discuss topics such as prayer, reading Scripture, and the sacraments? We would share our experiences and have the chance to talk through these sorts of Christian practices. What do you think? Would this sort of thing interest you?

Sue: Well, yes but I guess I'm not sure I understand what we'd do. What exactly would we do?

Leader: Well, we would meet weekly for a few weeks and we would use these Catholic materials for one-on-one mentoring. The booklet covers a different topic each week and it's very practical stuff. One week we would talk about daily prayer time and spend time praying together. Another week we look at how to deepen our sacramental life. Sue, you seem so open and eager to learn more about following Christ. I'd really enjoy the chance to get to know you and encourage you in your relationship with God.

Sue: That would be great.

Leader: Well, let's set up a time to meet. What days work best for you?

It's important to appropriately affirm people you invite when asking them to meet one-on-one for mentoring. Some may feel that if you are asking to meet with them about spiritual matters, then you must not think they are very good Christians. Of course this is not the case. Affirming them will help to overcome potential awkwardness.

Most important is that the leader prays about who God might be calling him to mentor. Jesus prayed about his disciples. In Luke's account of the calling of the twelve, Jesus spent the night praying to God before he called his disciples to him (cf. Luke 6:12). He was intentional about personally investing in Peter, James, and John and inviting them into special formative situations like the transfiguration. Pray for the person you are thinking of inviting and for their openness to this. Getting together with them for lunch or coffee and asking them to meet regularly within that social setting will make you both feel more comfortable.

For campus ministry or parish staff, asking may be easier than for peers. Campus ministers sometimes launch an apprenticeship ministry by offering one-on-one mentoring to a few students who might be well suited to mentoring their peers. After this initial group has experienced spiritual mentorship and grown in their sense that sharing faith is part of the life of a disciple, those interested can be prepared to mentor others.

It's usually best for the leader to invite his or her peers. This facilitates establishing a culture of spiritual mentoring. In the early stages of establishing this type of spiritual apprenticing, though, campus ministers and pastoral staff may want to invite students and parishioners, then assign them to appropriate mentors. This can alleviate the discomfort people feel about extending these invitations before a congregation becomes acquainted and comfortable with spiritual mentoring.

Praying for Your Discipleship Partner

Praying for your discipleship partner needs to become a regular part of your prayer routine, at least weekly, if not daily. Not only is interceding for them fruitful but it also gives God the opportunity to share his heart for them with you.

There will likely be times during your meetings with your discipleship partner that you may want to pray specifically for her. Sometimes all leaders feel at a loss for how to respond to something their disciples are saying, or stumped by some thorny problem they present. This is exactly the time to pray silently and fervently for the assistance of the Holy Spirit in serving this beloved child of God. Visualizing a tongue of fire or a white light above the head of your discipleship partner can help you stay focused on him or her while also praying for the Holy Spirit's intercession.

Most often you will pray using more "we" language, praying to God for his grace in both of your lives. This prayer can be made silently or vocally.

Preparing for Your One-on-One Meetings

You may meet one-on-one with more than one person. Using a sheet of paper to prepare for each person will allow you to make notes specific to that person's needs. You might write an additional question or two especially for your discipleship partner. You may also jot down numbers to note especially relevant discussion questions for your discipleship partner.

Make a file for each person you meet with or have a notebook with dividers so that you can keep track of how your session goes and what you actually did during your meetings. Then you can jot down where to start the next week and other pertinent notes.

Part of being a good mentor is being prepared and organized. Here is a quick list of steps for preparation:

- Pray for your discipleship partner and for the Holy Spirit's aid in your preparation.

- Allow time to read through the italicized notes, readings, questions and relevant appendices. Acquaint yourself with the material so you know how you will transition from one section to the next.

- Mark the questions you wish to prioritize by writing in the booklet or writing the question numbers on a separate piece of paper. Then if time gets away from you, you will be able to refer to these questions even if you are not able to get to every question.

- Make any copies that are needed. For example, in Week 5 you will need to print out the daily Scripture readings in advance for your discipleship partner.

Meeting and Setting Goals

For this initial meeting a public place can work if you have sufficient space and can speak without being overheard. A private room is best if it is a warm and inviting place that would not be threatening to the discipleship partner.

The goal of the first meeting is to get to know the person and establish a personal connection. You will do this by asking questions and listening a lot. You will need the Holy Spirit's guidance and help as you listen attentively and affirm through good eye contact and feedback. We all need the Holy Spirit's help to openly and authentically listen and to avoid jumping to conclusions and making judgments.

Below you will find many questions to help you navigate your first meeting and lead discussion. The questions will assist you in drawing out the discipleship partner so you can learn about them, establish points of relational commonality, and keep the conversation geared towards God.

The connection possible between people will vary tremendously. Sometimes a natural connection is made easily and quickly. For example, two people may find that they competed in track or another sport and share this interest; this can certainly help to create the beginning of a relationship of trust. Even if such a common point of interest is discovered and connection is made, the leader in this situation would want to take care not to let the whole meeting be sidetracked. Relational commonalities can be helpful but are not necessary. Most people feel human connection, if they simply have been listened to well, even if the two people conversing have little in common. We can't and shouldn't force connections that aren't there. God works wonders without them. We place our trust in the workings of the Holy Spirit to use us with or without common interests and experiences.

The following questions are a guide for you to review before an initial meeting with the discipleship partner. They will help you to appropriately direct the conversation. They are open-ended so you will naturally want to ask your own follow up questions. Spontaneity and interactive dialogue are necessary in the moment, but the more thoughtful and prayerful you are in your advance preparation, the better listener you will be and the more peace the Lord can convey through you during your meetings. You will be more relaxed and at ease with yourself and thus more free to listen and minister to them as the Lord leads.

In addition, the discipleship partner may want to ask you some of the same questions you ask *them. It's expected that you respond and establish a relationship. Just take care not to become sidetracked talking about yourself. Be natural and share about yourself but be aware of the temptation to make the time about you.*

Read through the following questions for your preparation. Notice the progression of questions goes from the factual to more spiritually oriented. You don't want to hurry this conversation but you also don't want to talk about your common love for "American Idol" for twenty-five minutes. You will likely have one to one and a half hours with them. Be sure to think through what questions you will ask that will help move the conversation to a deeper level. You will want to hear what they hope to gain from meeting one-on-one with someone and leave a little time for scheduling a second meeting.

Where are you from? What year are you in school? Where are you living? How is that working for you? How are your relationships with roommates?

For a freshman or new transfer student:
How do you like [name of school/city]? How's that whole adjustment going?

How are your classes this semester? Do you have ideas about what you want to study/major in?

It would be good to hear about what your religious or non-religious upbringing was like. Were you raised Catholic? What was that like? Did your parents take you to Mass every Sunday? Did you ever pray on your own or as a family? What was that like for you?

Did you go to religious education or CCD? What was that like for you?

Do you have any memories of God from your childhood? Did you have a connection to or belief in God throughout your childhood?

Were there any significant people or events in your life that had an impact on your relationship to God or your conception of God or religion?

Often after questions such as these there are plenty of gaps in information and openings to much larger conversations. Time demands that you ask some questions to help you and the person transition from reflecting on their past to the present.

What has your relationship to God/ conception of God been since college?

How did you find out about the discipleship program? What made you want to sign up for it? What are you hoping to gain from it?

Would you like to meet again next week? Was this a good time for you?

Take time to find a second meeting time. The goal should be to meet weekly for the nine sessions. (Meeting less frequently often leads to long gaps between meetings because of unexpected cancellations.) Share the weekly meeting goal and determine if this will work. Determine how long your meetings will/can be. Can you/they commit to one hour, one hour and fifteen minutes, or an hour and a half? The perfect time is either one hour and fifteen minutes or one hour and a half because these are discussions, not little lectures that can be condensed to a fifty minute class time. The extra fifteen to thirty minutes allows for personal catch-up in the beginning. With only 1 hour you miss out on a lot of good things for lack of time. But do what is possible for the two of you.

Closing Prayer

Offer to close your time together with a brief prayer. Even if you're in a public place, which is often comfortable for a first meeting, you can pray aloud discreetly. If you appear comfortable, you will set them at ease. Sample prayer:

> *Lord, thank you for our conversation today and the ways you have made it possible for us to experience your presence. Thank you for the ways you work in our lives. We thank you for your closeness to us during this time and at all times. We ask you to help us stay close to you for the rest of this day. We pray this through Christ, Our Lord. Amen.*

Important Moments in the

Process of Faith and Conversion

Week 1

Opening Prayer

Reading
General Directory for Catechesis

Leader: Following are several "important moments" in the process of faith and conversion. Your discipleship partner may or may not be able to identify with these. As your discipleship partner reads and discusses each, invite them to think about where he/she is and in what ways he/she relates or doesn't relate to what is read. Read the first two stages (a and b) and then pause to discuss them.

The Church uses the language of "important moments" in these paraphrases from the General Directory for Catechesis. This expression can be helpful, but one might also think he or she must be able to identify a particular moment. Sometimes "moment" can be understood as "season," "stage," "phase," etc. Other times "moment" is exactly how to describe our experience. Either way, the word can be loosely understood within a subjective context of each person's experience.

You will notice that the phrases "Good News of Jesus" and "Gospel" are used frequently. This might not be a helpful phrase for some people and may require clarification as you go along. Assuming someone understands the term can cause a gap in your communication and therefore in the fruitfulness of your discussion. On the other hand, addressing the term too early can bring up a pointed doctrinal question that can cause people to put up their guard and feel uneasy. Your goal is to help them discuss this organically, as part of the flow of conversation. This will be addressed more thoroughly in Week 2 but be aware of this possible communication gap and the need to introduce questions on this gently, for example: "This isn't a quiz so don't worry about a right answer but just so we are on the same page, how do you understand the 'Good News of Jesus?'" This may not be an issue at all.

Be discerning in navigating this session for the sake of the discipleship partner. If he is exploding with reaction to the first two "important moments" then don't feel obligated to address the final two important moments. If your partner is not full of responses to the first two important moments, give some time to the discussion questions that pertain to him but then be sure to move on to "Profession of Faith" and "Journeying towards Perfection" and discuss these. It is likely you will either spend the majority of the time on important moments a or b or you will jump to c and d and spend the majority of the time on them.

There is no need to cover all of this material. The point of the four important moments for the purpose of this session is to facilitate the discipleship partner's self-reflection and discussion with you of his searching, initial conversion, and path of discipleship to see if he wants to proceed with one-on-one mentoring. Note that if the discipleship partner related with important moment b, "conversion" you can skip the questions under a, "interest in the Good News" and go directly to the questions under "conversion."

a. Interest in the Good News of Jesus

This first moment pertains to the person who does not yet believe, is indifferent, or practices other religions. The first moment is one in which there is born an interest in the Good News of Jesus Christ (the Gospel). An initial interest is born as a result of a first proclamation of the Gospel; the means of being initially exposed to the Good News of Jesus Christ are endless: through the many people we encounter in life, through books, the events of our lives, the sacraments, Scripture, etc. Yet, in this first moment, no firm decision of faith has been made. This first movement of the human spirit towards faith is already a fruit of God's grace (that supernatural assistance which moves and aids the human heart).[1]

b. Conversion

The first moment of interest in the Gospel requires a period of searching. This period of searching is then to be transformed into a firm decision to put one's faith in God through Jesus Christ. This decision of faith must be a considered and mature one. This period of searching, guided by the Holy Spirit and the proclamation of the Good News of Jesus, prepares the way for "initial" conversion. Though this conversion is certainly "initial," it brings with it adherence to Christ and the desire to walk in his footsteps. This important moment is often referred to as the "fundamental option" because it is the basis for the whole Christian life of the Lord's disciple.[2]

1. Do you have any initial comments or questions?

2. What resonated with you? Or what seemed strange or unfamiliar to you?

3. Can you identify with either of these stages?

[1] Congregation for the Clergy, <u>General Directory for Catechesis,</u> United States Catholic Conference (Washington, D.C., 1997) paragraph 56, pages 49-50. These "important moments" as described are paraphrased for use in one-on-one discussions.

[2] Ibid.

Interest in the Good News

4. If you identify most with "Interest in the Good News," how would you describe your present interest?

5. How would you describe your present period of searching?

6. What are some of the things that you feel are keeping you from making a firm decision?

Conversion

7. If you relate with the "initial conversion" moment and feel that your period of searching has moved (or is moving) to a firm decision, how would you describe your experience of "initial" conversion? Was it radical, more gradual, or somewhere in the middle?

8. Did God use a key event, person, or thing to call you to relationship to Christ?

9. If you are unable to identify a specific moment of "initial" conversion, how would you describe the development of your personal relationship with God through Jesus?

10. What went into you having the faith you received so gradually and beautifully?

11. Did anything help you make a firm decision to follow Christ?

Leader: Don't allow questions 3 and 4 below addressing "profession of faith" to cause confusion in your discussion. There is no right or wrong answer. Rather, let your discussion focus on the main point of the question: what does it mean or indicate about a person's faith in Christ when they have reached the point at which they are ready to make an explicit profession of their faith? Then if possible apply the concept of a profession of faith for reflection on their lives via these questions. Maybe they realized that they had reached this point when they were put on the spot about a moral decision they had made that was different from their friends. Explaining to their friends how their relationship with Christ had changed them is an example of what might have been an unofficial type of "profession of faith."

c. Profession of faith Abandonment of self to Jesus Christ arouses in believers a desire to know him more profoundly and to identify with him. Catechesis initiates them in knowledge of faith and apprenticeship in the Christian life, thereby promoting a spiritual journey which brings about a "progressive change in outlook and morals." This is achieved in sacrifices and in challenges, as well as in the joys which God gives in abundance. The disciple of Jesus Christ is then ready to make an explicit, living and fruitful profession of faith.[3]

1. How would you describe your own journey of change with regard to outlook and morals as a result of following Christ? What sacrifices and challenges has this presented to you? Please explain.

2. Have you experienced the "joys which God gives in abundance" as result of following Christ?

3. The expression "profession of faith" sounds official, and it is the church's official language. What did or would it mean to you to make "a profession of faith?" What do you think a "profession of faith" would say or indicate?

Once you have established a shared definition of profession of faith:

4. Why would a "profession of faith" be an important moment in the process of faith and conversion?

5. Have you had opportunities to grow in experience and knowledge of how to pray, read Scripture, receive the sacraments, partake in Christian community, and share your faith, etc. (apprenticeship in the Christian life)? Is this something that would interest you?

6. Have you had opportunities to grow in knowledge of Catholic Christianity? Is this something that would interest you?

d. Journeying towards Perfection The basic maturity which gives rise to the profession of faith is not the final point in the process of continuing conversion. The profession of baptismal faith is but the foundation of a spiritual building which is destined to grow. The baptized, moved always by the Spirit, nourished by the sacraments, by prayer and by the practice of charity, and assisted by multiple forms

---

[3] Congregation for the Clergy, General Directory for Catechesis, paragraph 56.

of ongoing education in the faith, seeks to realize the desire of Christ: "Be perfect as your heavenly Father is perfect." This is the call to the fullness of perfection which is addressed to all the baptized.[4]

1. **Does anything strike you from this last "important moment" in the process of faith and conversion?**

Leader: The duration of the first session will vary for different people. For some, the session could take the entire hour and a half. Others, who happened to discuss these matters in "Meeting and Setting Goals," might find that you have completed Week 1 with time to spare. If this is the case, feel free to do the first part of Week 2 (introductory paragraphs and introduction of the Wheel). This will follow nicely from Week 1 and set you up well for the rest of Week 2 for your next meeting. Even if you did cover some of these matters in your opening conversations in "Meeting and Setting Goals," this session invites the discipleship partner into deeper reflection on their interior conversion. This is an extremely important step for them. It will help them to see how much God has pursued and loved them and it will also make them better witnesses since they will have a better sense of their own faith story.

Closing Prayer

---

[4] Congregation for the Clergy, General Directory for Catechesis, paragraph 56.

Life in Christ – Being a Child of God

Week 2

"So if anyone is in Christ, there is a new creation:
everything old has passed away;
see, everything has become new!"

2 Corinthians 5:17

Leader: By this time it would be best if your one-on-one meetings could take place in a private room or other location conducive to deeper, focused conversation. Praying aloud together and discussing faith topics is personal and private. People are often more at ease and willing to pray aloud or share intimately if they're certain they cannot be overheard or observed.

Opening Prayer

Introduction

Leader: Please ask the discipleship partner to read the following paragraphs aloud.

In the last session we discussed "initial" conversion as an important moment in the process of faith and conversion. As was stated, "this 'fundamental option' is the basis for the whole Christian life of the Lord's disciple." The word disciple comes from the Latin word for student. Jesus' followers were his students. That means we too have to ask: How do we live as a student of Jesus? What does a disciple do?

Becoming a disciple of Christ does not happen accidentally, but intentionally and purposefully. As we read in Week 2 from the <u>General Directory for Catechesis</u>, "Abandonment of self to Jesus Christ arouses in believers a desire to know him more profoundly and to identify with him. Catechesis initiates them in knowledge of faith and apprenticeship in the Christian life…" To become a disciple, we need help in being intentional!

Throughout Christian history those who wanted to become Jesus' disciples or learn more about following him apprenticed themselves to those who had walked further on the Way. This apprenticeship in the Christian life is essential in the process of becoming a disciple. We must be as intentional about it as we would anything else we want to accomplish, or it won't happen. A wanna-be plumber must learn how to run copper tubing, operate a torch, and install a sink. That is why he apprentices with a plumbing professional. How else can he learn? So, too, must we humble ourselves to learn the way of the disciple of Jesus.

1. What do you think an apprenticeship as a disciple of Christ would look like?

2. What practices, habits, and mindsets do you think would make up your apprenticeship?

3. How would you learn what a disciple does?

4. What situations could you seek out or establish to help you try to do those things, too?

The Wheel

Leader: Here you will present the Wheel to give your discipleship partner a grid for what the upcoming sessions will cover. In language natural to you, explain how Christ being the hub or center of the Wheel represents Christ becoming the center of our lives through initial and ongoing interior conversion. Scripture passages follow that teach us how we are made new in Christ and how through him we have become sons and daughters of God. We pray that these truths would help us to better walk in the truth of who we are and help us to fall more personally in love with God who loved us so much that he sent his Son so that we might become his children.

Briefly point out the other aspects and habits that make up the Wheel. If they had mentioned any of these aspects earlier in your discussion on Christian apprenticeship, you will want to tie that in here. You will discuss the parts of the Wheel in greater detail (i.e., why they're placed where they are, etc.) in the upcoming sessions. For now, it's important to note that Christ at the center of the Wheel represents Christ at the center of our lives. That is what you will talk about today.

Scripture for Memorization

Leader: The Scripture passages for memorization in each session correspond with the habit or aspect of discipleship of the Wheel. At the least, ask your partner to read aloud these verses that go with the Wheel. If your discipleship partner seems up to the challenge, encourage them to memorize one or both of these verses each week. You can offer to do it with them if you haven't done much Scripture memorization. Time isn't an issue because it is a discipline that can be done as you walk between classes. Encourage your discipleship partner to do this daily so that the Word seeps into their hearts and minds, rather than rushing to memorize before your meeting. Checking in on verses and sharing fruits of Scripture memorization adds a great dimension to mentoring. It grounds you and them in the Word of God!

2 Corinthians 5:17
"So if anyone is in Christ, there is a new creation: everything old has passed away; see, everything has become new!"

Galatians 2:20
"I have been crucified with Christ; and it is no longer I who live, but it is Christ who lives in me. And the life I now live in the flesh I live by faith in the Son of God, who loved me and gave himself for me."

Reading

Leader: You have just introduced the Wheel and talked about the need to be intentional about becoming Christ's disciple. Now we're changing the angle of this reflection by talking about divine filiation, our relationship as sons and daughters of the Father, God. This reflection makes sense here because Jesus is the Way to the Father. He came to bring us to the Father and to invite us into communion, a blessed friendship with the Trinity. Getting closer to Jesus brings us close to the Father. As disciples of Jesus, we walk in this world as beloved, children of God. This truth is part of the foundation of the hub of the Wheel (Christ the Center).

Leader: Ask the discipleship partner to read the following introduction and Scripture passage aloud.

As a disciple of Christ, understanding your identity as a child of God and trying to live as a child of God is foundational for living as "new creations" and continuously allowing the old to pass away (2 Corinthians 5:17). St. Paul's letter to the Romans explains this gift we receive through Christ - our divine "filiation." (Filius is Latin for "son," filia for "daughter." "Filiation" describes our relationship as sons and daughters of God, our loving Father through Christ, who made us children of God.)   Knowledge of filiation can be the source of the courage it takes to live as "new creations."

Romans 8: 14-17

¹⁴For all who are led by the Spirit of God are children of God. ¹⁵For you did not receive a spirit of slavery to fall back into fear, but you have received a spirit of adoption. When we cry, 'Abba! Father!' ¹⁶it is that very Spirit bearing witness with our spirit that we are children of God, ¹⁷and if children, then heirs, heirs of God and joint heirs with Christ—if, in fact, we suffer with him so that we may also be glorified with him.

1. We might think of God our Father in terms of the perfect, ideal mother and father, combined into one though immeasurably greater than we can imagine. What attributes do ideal parents have? Have you thought of God being the one who fulfills this ideal? How does this affect your image of God?

2. Have you ever thought of yourself as a beloved daughter of God or a beloved son of God? What does that description of who you are in relation to God mean for you?

3. St. Paul describes the spirit of adoption that we have received from Christ in contrast to the spirit of slavery or fear. What do you think it would be like to be a slave in a house in ancient Israel or Rome as opposed to a son or daughter? What based on that would you say are the characteristics of a spirit of slavery? Why do you think St. Paul describes being a daughter and son of God in this way?

4. Have you ever felt enslaved or fearful? What was that like? How can a person's relationship as son or daughter of God through Christ change the nature of these struggles?

5. St. Paul clearly identified and experienced himself as a beloved son of God. We can hear in the text that he himself had cried out to God – "Abba, Father" - probably in times of suffering. (He makes no secret of his trials, especially in 2 Corinthians.) Jesus also modeled this for us before his death as he cried out

to God, the Father: "Abba, why have you forsaken me?" What are some ways of relating intimately to God? What are some ways God might be inviting you to relate more intimately with Him?

Catechism of the Catholic Church

Leader: The following readings from the Catechism of the Catholic Church will spur further reflection on this concept of divine filiation.

> 305 Jesus asks for childlike abandonment to the providence of our heavenly Father who takes care of his children's smallest needs: "Therefore do not be anxious, saying, "What shall we eat?" or "What shall we drink?"... Your heavenly Father knows that you need them all. But seek first his kingdom and his righteousness, and all these things shall be yours as well."[1]

The following from the <u>Catechism of the Catholic Church</u> reflects on "Give us this day our daily bread" from the Our Father.

> 2830 "*Our bread*": The Father who gives us life cannot but give us the nourishment life requires - all appropriate goods and blessings, both material and spiritual. In the Sermon on the Mount, Jesus insists on the filial trust that cooperates with our Father's providence.[2] He is not inviting us to idleness,[3] but wants to relieve us from nagging worry and preoccupation. Such is the filial surrender of the children of God:

> To those who seek the kingdom of God and his righteousness, he has promised to give all else besides. Since everything indeed belongs to God, he who possesses God wants for nothing, if he himself is not found wanting before God.[4]

1. **What struck you from these paragraphs?**

2. **Why are children used as a good example of abandonment and trust?**

3. **How does anxiety and worry affect you? How does it affect your relationships? How does it affect your relationship with God?**

---

[1] Matthew 6: 31-33; cf. 10:29-31.
[2] Cf. Mt 6:25-34.
[3] Cf. 2 Thess 3:6-13.
[4] St. Cyprian, *De Dom. orat.* 21: PL 4, 534A.

4. How can we begin to surrender ourselves and trust God, Our Father? Besides God's grace working this in us, what are some practical steps we can take to live a life of trust and surrender?

5. Can you think of people in your life who model this filial trust and surrender?

Closing Prayer

A Rich Sacramental Life

Week 3

*"And like living stones
be yourselves built into a spiritual house,
to be a holy priesthood, to offer spiritual sacrifices
acceptable to God through Jesus Christ."*

1 Peter 2:5

Opening Prayer

The Wheel

Leader: Invite your discipleship partner to refer back to the Wheel in Week 2. You will do this each week. Looking at the actual illustration as you discuss the aspect or habit of discipleship for the week will help keep the big picture in mind and aid in your brief discussion of the Wheel.

1. **Where is the sacramental life in relationship to "Christ" the hub? Why might "the sacraments" be centrally located around the hub of the Wheel?**

Scripture for Memorization

1 Peter 2:5
"And like living stones be yourselves built into a spiritual house, to be a holy priesthood, to offer spiritual sacrifices acceptable to God through Jesus Christ."

Acts 2:41a-42
"So those who received his word were baptized . . . And they devoted themselves to the apostles' teaching and fellowship, to the breaking of bread and the prayers."

Leader: The goals of this session are:

- *To help the discipleship partner reflect on his/her Baptism through the Scripture from Romans. The discipleship partner should be able to connect the conversion of heart she has experienced with her sacramental conversion of Baptism (St. Augustine's distinction). Once the heart has been converted and cleansed of sin, there begins an untying of the believer's baptismal graces, in which she begins walking in God's grace and living out the call to love and serve God and others.*

- *To provide space for reflection on how we are freed from sin through baptism and yet death to sin remains a constant struggle. When appropriate sharing your own struggle with sin and weakness and what helped you though it may set your discipleship partner at ease. It may also assist them in seeing that being a Christian includes intense struggles through which God builds in us humility, trust, and dependence on him.*

- *This discussion of Baptism should naturally lead into the next discussion of Eucharist and Reconciliation, the two sacraments we can receive frequently to renew and increase Christ's life in us, begun at Baptism. The emphasis in your discussion of the readings from the <u>Catechism of the Catholic Church</u> for Eucharist and Confession should be the personal encounter we can have with Christ through these sacraments and the abundant grace available to us in them. A perfect theological understanding of the sacraments isn't necessary or even possible at this point.*

- *In your preparation, be sure to outline how much time you think you will spend on each section so that you can get to the readings from the <u>Catechism of the Catholic Church</u>. For example, you may spend ten minutes talking initially, five minutes with the opening prayer, forty minutes on the reading from Romans, thirty minutes on the <u>Catechism of the Catholic Church</u>, leaving you with five minutes for closing prayer in a one hour and a half session.*

Reading

Romans 6: 1-11

¹What then are we to say? Should we continue in sin in order that grace may abound? ²By no means! How can we who died to sin go on living in it? ³Do you not know that all of us who have been baptized into Christ Jesus were baptized into his death? ⁴Therefore we have been buried with him by baptism into death, so that, just as Christ was raised from the dead by the glory of the Father, so we too might walk in newness of life. ⁵For if we have been united with him in a death like his, we will certainly be united with him in a resurrection like his. ⁶We know that our old self was crucified with him so that the body of sin might be destroyed, and we might no longer be enslaved to sin. ⁷For whoever has died is freed from sin. ⁸But if we have died with Christ, we believe that we will also live with him. ⁹We know that Christ, being raised from the dead, will never die again; death no longer has dominion over him. ¹⁰The death he died, he died to sin, once for all; but the life he lives, he lives to God. ¹¹So you also must consider yourselves dead to sin and alive to God in Christ Jesus.

1. **Take a moment to circle the phrases that describe the fruits or positive results of being buried with Christ by baptism into death. Now underline all the phrases that have to do with dying with Christ or sin.**

2. How does St. Paul describe baptism here? What does Christ do in the believer through Baptism?

3. Imagine a full immersion Baptism in which a person walks down into a font is baptized and then walks up and out of the font a baptized Catholic. What do these baptismal actions symbolize? (Use St. Paul's language in the Scripture here and your own.)

4. St. Paul emphasizes Christ's death in this passage. Why do you think this is his emphasis? What does St. Paul say we are freed from?

5. The Catechism of the Catholic Church teaches in paragraphs 1263-64 that through Baptism all sins are forgiven, original sin and all personal sins as well as all punishment for sin. Yet certain temporal consequences of sin remain in the baptized, such as suffering, illness, death, frailties inherent in life such as weaknesses of character, as well as our general inclination towards sin.

   Given this, how would you convince yourself and others that Christ's death for our sin was the greatest gift God could give us? What would St. Paul say to this?

6. In verse 6, St. Paul used the phrases "enslaved to sin" and "freed from sin." Do you ever feel that you lack freedom with regard to the struggle against sin? How do you deal with this struggle?

7. The Catechism of the Catholic Church paragraphs 1272 and 1121 state that Baptism seals the Christian with the indelible (permanent) mark (character) of his belonging to Christ. This remains forever as a positive disposition for grace, a promise and guarantee of divine protection, and as a vocation (call) to divine worship and to service of the Church. No sin can erase this mark, even if sin prevents Baptism from bearing the fruits of salvation.

   What strikes you about the above teaching on Baptism? What does this permanent nature of the seal of Baptism mean to you?

8. Baptism is an unrepeatable sacrament. What sacraments can the Catholic receive regularly? How do these sacraments strengthen the grace of Baptism?

Catechism of the Catholic Church

1391 *Holy Communion augments our union with Christ.* The principal fruit of receiving the Eucharist in Holy Communion is an intimate union with Christ Jesus. Indeed, the Lord said: "He who eats my flesh and drinks my blood abides in me, and I in him."[1] Life in Christ has its foundation in the Eucharistic banquet: "As the living Father sent me, and I live because of the Father, so he who eats me will live because of me."[2]

1392 What material food produces in our bodily life, Holy Communion wonderfully achieves in our spiritual life. Communion with the flesh of the risen Christ, a flesh "given life and giving life through the Holy Spirit,"[3] preserves, increases, and renews the life of grace received at Baptism. This growth in Christian life needs the nourishment of Eucharistic Communion, the bread for our pilgrimage until the moment of death, when it will be given to us as viaticum.[4]

1. **What strikes you from these paragraphs on the Eucharist?**

2. **What does it mean that Christ is really present in the Eucharist?**

3. **What are the fruits of reception of Christ in the Eucharist? Has this been your experience?**

4. **How can you to grow closer to Christ through the Eucharist?**

1457 ...Anyone who is aware of having committed a mortal sin must not receive Holy Communion, even if he experiences deep contrition, without having first received sacramental absolution, unless he has a grave reason for receiving Communion and there is no possibility of going to confession. 1857 ..."Mortal sin is sin whose object is grave matter and which is also committed with full knowledge and deliberate consent."[5]

1458 Without being strictly necessary, confession of everyday faults (venial sins) is nevertheless strongly recommended by the Church. Indeed the regular confession of our venial sins helps us form our conscience, fight against evil tendencies, let ourselves be healed by Christ and progress in the life of the Spirit. By receiving more frequently through this sacrament the gift of the Father's mercy, we are spurred to be merciful as he is merciful.[6]

[1] Jn 6:56.
[2] John 6: 57
[3] PO 5
[4] Viaticum refers to Eucharist given to a dying person or one in danger of death.
[5] Cf. Council of Trent (1551): DS 1647; 1661; CIC, can. 916; CCEO, can. 711.
[6] Cf. Lk 6:36.

1. How does the teaching in paragraph 1457 relate with the discussion above of the real presence of Christ in the Eucharist? How does the Sacrament of Reconciliation help one to prepare for more intimate reception of Holy Communion? Has this been your experience?

2. What are the fruits of regular confession?

3. It is not uncommon to feel hesitant, nervous, or even fearful of Reconciliation. Is this or has this been your experience? What are some ways to focus on Christ during this sacrament?

4. How might you make the Sacrament of Reconciliation a regular part of your life as Christ's disciple?

Leader: the discipleship partner may desire a fuller understanding of why Catholics have the Sacrament of Confession. You may find it helpful to review paragraphs 1446-1448 in the <u>Catechism of the Catholic Church</u> which can be found in Appendix B. You may want to refer them to these paragraphs. You might consider inviting him/her to go to Confession with you at your parish or Newman Center. You will want to point out the guide to the Sacrament of Reconciliation in Appendix C and the examination of conscience available in Appendix D. You may also share practices you have, such as praying beforehand or writing notes from which you talk to the priest.

Closing Prayer

Personal Prayer
Week 4

*"Do not worry about anything, but in everything
by prayer and supplication with thanksgiving
let your requests be made known to God.
And the peace of God, which surpasses all understanding,
will guard your hearts and your minds in Christ Jesus."*

Philippians 4: 6-7

Opening Prayer

Introduction

Leader: The following questions are meant to set up the discussion on personal prayer within the context of relationship. These questions provide a good introduction to the topic. For question 2 give your discipleship partner a moment to think of their closest friends or family members and their attributes. This will set up the exercise well so that they can then apply these reflections to their relationship with God.

Regular personal prayer is the Christian's most vital link to Christ. Without regular personal prayer, a person's relationship with God will lack roots. Like the seeds sewn on rocky path; their growth will be limited or cease completely. As St. Bernard said, "He who does not advance, falls back."[1] Two weeks are therefore dedicated to the priority of prayer to allow for adequate groundwork, growth in conviction about the importance of this habit of a disciple, and time to experience prayer with the leader.

1. Think of the people you know (from your dorm, classes, work place, or neighborhood) at whom you would simply wave or acknowledge in some way.

    What kind of a relationship do you have with acquaintances or persons to whom you simply wave as you pass? How do these relationships compare to those with people with whom you would stop and talk?

2. What word or two would you use to describe your relationship with these two groups?

3. Now think of the most intimate relationships you have with friends, a boyfriend/girlfriend, a spouse, or family members. Choosing one or two of those people, write down or think of 3 or 4 attributes that positively describe them. How do you know those things about them?

4. How did you grow close to those people?

5. From your perspective, what makes for closeness or intimacy?

1 Epist., 34, 1; 91, 3; 254, 4.

6. Applying your above reflections to your life as a Christian, where would you place your current relationship with God in terms of closeness on the following spectrum? Why?

No relationship   Acquaintance   Friend   Good friend   Close friend   Best friend

0-------------------1-------------------2-------------------3-------------------4-------------------5

7. What do you think of when I say, "prayer"? How would you define prayer?

8. What has been your experience of prayer? What ways have you prayed? Have there been times when you have felt moved to turn your heart towards God or to pray? What was that like?

Leader: One way to transition from the above introductory discussion to the following reading from the Gospel of Mark is to point out that God is always the initiator. When we have a good thought or two or find ourselves turning to him, we are actually responding to God's initiating. Realizing this is exciting and moves us to want to tune into him who is always tuned into us so that our relationship can grow.

The Wheel

Leader: Take a minute to refer to the Wheel in Week 2. One way to remember the vertical position of Prayer and Scripture on the Wheel is that they point "up" to heaven and are important habits of discipleship. Without them the inner circle of the sacraments will be less fruitful and our connection to the hub of Christ will weaken. It is sometimes said in reference to the Wheel that disciples need a strong vertical pull in their lives. This section only needs to take 1-2 minutes. Pedagogically it is helpful for setting up the session.

1. What significance might the position of prayer on the Wheel have from illustrating discipleship?

Scripture for Memorization

Philippians 4:6-7

"Do not worry about anything, but in everything by prayer and supplication with thanksgiving let your requests be made known to God. And the peace of God, which surpasses all understanding, will guard your hearts and your minds in Christ Jesus."

Matthew 6:6

"But whenever you pray, go into your room and shut the door and pray to your Father who is in secret; and your Father who sees in secret will reward you."

Reading

Mark 1: 34-39

Leader: This Scripture shows our first model for prayer – Jesus! He responded fully and perfectly to God's promptings. Jesus was so close to his Father he was able to say that they are/ were one! Prayer was Jesus' main means of maintaining this closeness with the Father.

³⁴And he cured many who were sick with various diseases, and cast out many demons; and he would not permit the demons to speak, because they knew him. ³⁵ In the morning, while it was still very dark, he got up and went out to a deserted place, and there he prayed. ³⁶And Simon and his companions hunted for him. ³⁷When they found him, they said to him, 'Everyone is searching for you.' ³⁸He answered, 'Let us go on to the neighbouring towns, so that I may proclaim the message there also; for that is what I came out to do.' ³⁹And he went throughout Galilee, proclaiming the message in their synagogues and casting out demons.

1. **What can we learn from this passage about Jesus' prayer life?**

2. **Though we know Jesus' communion with God our Father never ceased (he truly did as St. Paul exhorts, "to pray without ceasing"), why do you think Jesus set aside specific times for prayer? Why do we need to go to a "deserted place" and set aside regular time for prayer?**

3. **If you have ever tried to pray regularly, what were the fruits of it? Did you notice any difference in your life or in how you handled life when you were praying regularly versus when you are not?**

Leader: Below is a summation from the Catechism of the Catholic Church and writings of Catholic saints on three major expressions of prayer: vocal, meditative, and contemplative. They define ways we pray and they give us a vision for how God means for us to grow through prayer as it leads us to greater oneness with him until we are ultimately one with him in heaven. The saints traveled down this pathway of vocal, mental prayer, and contemplative prayer as they grew in relationship to God. Just as God guided the saints, so he wants to guide us. Read these paragraphs aloud together and discuss the questions that follow.

Vocal Prayer

A vocal prayer gives expression of our prayer in the physical world. The Holy Mass contains many vocal prayers (e.g., the Our Father). Other vocal prayers are the Hail Mary, the Glory Be and the Church's Liturgy of the Hours prayed by religious and lay people around the world. St. Teresa of Avila suggests that vocal and mental prayer are inseparable: "If while I utter a prayer I carefully consider its meaning and pay more attention to what I am saying to God than to the words themselves, this is both mental and vocal prayer."

Meditation or Mental Prayer

When we meditate on the sacred Scriptures, writings of the saints, or other spiritual books, we engage our thoughts, imagination, emotions, and desires. "Mobilizing these faculties is necessary in order to deepen our convictions of faith, prompt the conversion of our heart, and strengthen our will to follow Christ."[2] When we meditate on what we read we make it our own by confronting or considering it ourselves. St. Teresa of Avila defines mental prayer this way: "Prayer in my opinion is nothing else than a close sharing between friends; it means taking time frequently to be alone with him who we know loves us." Through prayer, God increases his love and joy within us and gives us the grace to know ourselves and the goodness of God continually at work within us.

1. **What struck you from the readings on vocal and mental prayer?**

2. **What do you think of St. Teresa's definition of mental prayer? Is this similar to or different from your conception of prayer?**

Contemplative Prayer

St. Teresa of Avila who describes four degrees of prayer says that during contemplation the soul "understands that it is enjoying a good in which are gathered together all goods, but this good is incomprehensible. All the senses are occupied in this joy in such a way that none is free to be taken up with any other exterior or interior thing."[3] This form of prayer is one for which you prepare yourself through mental prayer but essentially it is a gift, a grace from God. Contemplation is God moving us into greater intimacy with Him. We prepare ourselves to accept in great humility by making the effort to be in

[2] Ibid., 2708.

[3] Kavanaugh, Kieran and Rodriguez, Otilio. <u>The Collected Works of St. Teresa of Avila, Vol. I, The Book of Her Life. Spiritual Testimonies, Soliloquies</u>, page 157, ICS Publications, Washington, D.C., 1987.

God's presence, in loving union. While some saints and others experienced the gift of contemplative prayer consistently, others experience but moments of contemplation.

3. Have you ever had an encounter with Christ that raised within you a strong desire to pray or be with God? What was that like? What impact, if any, did that experience have on you, on your prayer at Mass, or your vocal prayer, such as the Our Father?

Closing Prayer

Leader: For the next session, also dedicated to personal prayer, the discipleship partner will need to bring his/her class/work/personal schedule in order to help him/her devise a personal daily prayer plan. Be sure to tell them now and remind by an e-mail or call before your meeting.

Introduction to Praying with Scripture

Week 5

"But whenever you pray,
go into your room and shut the door
and pray to your Father who is in secret;
and your Father who sees in secret will reward you."

Matthew 6:6

Leader: This session includes a twenty to thirty minute section in which you and the discipleship partner will pray aloud together. You will want to meet in a place where you and the discipleship partner will feel comfortable praying aloud. Meeting in a chapel can work well or in an office space where you know you will have privacy.

You will want to go to www.usccb.org/nab on the United States Conference of Catholic Bishops' website. This is the web address for the list of daily readings for the current liturgical year. Print out a couple weeks of the Sunday and daily readings for your discipleship partner. (You don't need to print the text of the readings, just the Scripture citations.) Bring this with you to give to him/her at the end of this session.

Opening Prayer

Introduction

1. Many Christians have described prayer as simply "focused attention." What is it like when someone gives you focused attention? How does that make you feel?

2. What is it like for you to focus on another person? Are you aware of doing it? Do you ever very intentionally focus your attention on someone when you would perhaps not naturally?

3. What are the positive effects or fruits of focused attention on relationships?

4. A wise monk said, "Until you believe prayer is the best use of your time, you will not make time for prayer." What truth does this quote seek to uncover? What impedes your prayer? How does this quote speak to you?

5. What is prayer for? Why do you want a regular prayer life?

Reading

Leader: In order to leave the majority of time for the explanation of prayer and actually praying with your discipleship partner, be careful not to spend too much time on the quotes below from St. Teresa of Avila. Ask your discipleship partner to read the following paragraphs aloud.

The <u>Catechism of the Catholic Church</u> teaches that "we cannot pray 'at all times' if we do not pray at specific times, consciously willing it."[1] St. Teresa of Avila says, "Take my advice, and let no one mislead you by pointing out any other way than prayer."[2]

Implementing daily prayer into your life can be a lot like trying to stick with a new exercise program. Difficult! St. Teresa of Avila says this is how one must begin well:

> I maintain that this is the chief point; in fact that everything depends on people having a great and a most resolute determination never to halt until they reach their journey's end, happen what may, whatever the consequences are, cost what it will, let who will blame them, whether they reach the goal or die on the road, or lose heart to bear the trials they encounter, or the earth itself goes to pieces beneath their feet.[3]

> …if people don't abandon it [prayer], they may believe that prayer will bring them to the harbor of light. And how right the devil is to direct his attacks so that the soul give up prayer! The traitor knows that he has lost the soul that practices prayer perseveringly and that all the falls he helps it to take assist it afterward, through the goodness of God, to make a great leap forward in the Lord's service. No wonder he's so concerned![4]

1. **What strikes you from the above quotes?**

2. **Why do you think that St. Teresa exhorts us so intensely to begin the life of prayer with "a most resolute determination"? What is the pay-off of prayer for her?**

3. **What might be your greatest challenge as you begin to implement a regular prayer time? How might the devil direct his attacks so that you give up prayer?**

Leader: Set aside at least twenty minutes to do mental prayer with your discipleship partner. You will need at least fifteen minutes prior to talk through the method for prayer below. The following explanation may help you as you describe it to them.

[1] <u>Catechism of the Catholic Church</u>, 2697. Also cf. 1 Thessalonians 5:17.
[2] St. Teresa of Avila, <u>The Way of Perfection</u>, 128.
[3] Zimmerman, Fr. Benedict. <u>The Way of Perfection</u>, page 125, Tan Books, Rockford, ILL, 1997.
[4] Kavanaugh and Rodriguez, <u>The Book of Her Life</u>, page 166.

There are many methods and styles of meditation and prayer. The following is a very simple one recommended by St. Francis de Sales among countless other Catholics. It involves engaging the various faculties of the soul and mobilizing them to know God more and to love him more. Your faculties include:

- *your intellect or your mind, with its capacity for reasoning, memory and imagination;*

- *your affections or your heart, which includes all feelings and emotions;*

- *your will, which includes your desire and determination.*

"Mobilizing" implies effort on our part – the effort to pause, sit with something, and think about why it struck us. This requires effort since, as in any relationship, we are not always flying high with affection for God. We do not need to fake affections or feelings. God knows the difference! There are times we are called to rouse ourselves spiritually and other times when we might be called to "be still."[5]

St. Francis de Sales recommended that we let our hearts buzz around like a bee looking for the sweet nectar that is attracting us in God's Word or a spiritual work. If something moves us, we should pay attention and remain with it, conversing with God about it until we have sucked all the nectar we can. When the nectar is gone, we should gently and lovingly continue buzzing around till we find more nectar.

In prayer, we should avoid trying to accomplish a goal of reading a certain number of pages or even paragraphs. This is counter-productive to the object of prayer which is a loving conversation with God. We want to be faithful to the Holy Spirit by pausing when we feel drawn to something or to allow God to draw something to our attention. Sometimes we feel a visitation from the Lord, or that he is putting a word on our hearts. Only pausing will allow that to take root in our hearts.

In a personal prayer time, one might set aside 15 minutes for slow spiritual reading with devotion and then pause to go back, meditating and conversing with the Lord on things you underlined for another 15 minutes. Or you might decide to pause immediately after finding "nectar."

Review "A Method for Prayer" below with your discipleship partner **by reading through the steps BEFORE entering into the prayer time together.** It is important to set this exercise up well and use the set-up as a teaching opportunity. This helps them learn a simple method

---

[5] Psalm 46: 10.

they can use for their prayer. Allowing ample set-up time will help you both feel less nervous about praying aloud, something many Catholics are unaccustomed to doing.

If you are in a Chapel, you may wish to kneel for the preparation and then be seated for the reading.

A Method for Prayer

Preparation

Have a pen or pencil with you so you can mark the verses from Scripture that strike you.

1. Take a moment for silence and recall God's presence in you.

2. Pray aloud together this common pre-meditation Catholic prayer and the following prayer to the Holy Spirit. When doing this alone, be sure to pause as you feel led to do so.

My Lord and my God, I firmly believe that you are here; that you see me, that your hear me. I adore you with profound reverence; I beg your pardon for my sins, and the grace to make this time of prayer fruitful. My Immaculate Mother, Saint Joseph my father and lord, my guardian angel, intercede for me.

Come, Holy Spirit, open our hearts and minds to your presence in our hearts as we read. Help us to desire to know God, our Father, and awaken our hearts to love him and talk with him.

Reading and Meditation

3. Read Psalm 103 antiphonally together. This means that each of you reads a stanza while the other listens. At the end of a stanza, the first reader stops, and then the other proceeds reading the next stanza. As you read, you may wish to mark verses that stand out to you. After you read the Psalm aloud once, read it aloud a second time antiphonally, but read the opposite stanzas, the ones you didn't already read. When you have finished reading, pause in silence, returning to look at the stanzas that most stood out to you.

4. After you have read, take a minute in silence to reflect on one of the verses you marked. What do you learn about God or about yourself from that verse? How does that truth strike you? Why did that verse stand out to you? What is the impact on you of the truth you encounter in these words? How do you relate to the verse or words right now?

5. Take turns conversing aloud with God about the verse(s) that you marked and on which you meditated. After the first person prays about her verse(s), then the second person may add to that or echo something in her prayer and/or choose to begin conversing right away about the verses on which she meditated. Either way, the second person should eventually pray about something on which they meditated so each has a chance to practice conversation based on their reflections.

6. The goal is to press into God together to follow the Holy Spirit's movement in the Word and in each other. When the other person prays aloud, pray with them interiorly. That will allow you to benefit and share in their conversation with God. Try not to worry about what you sound like. What pleases God is a desire to please him. Agree to turn off the internal editing! After the second person has prayed the process repeats itself. The first person, if he/she feels like moving to a new verse, converses with God about another verse(s) that stood out to him/her and then the second person continues the conversation with the same verse or different ones that she marked.

7. The goals are to:

   a. use your INTELLECT (reason, memory, and/or imagination) to note what verse(s) strike you and to think about them;

   b. rouse your AFFECTIONS, your heart, feelings, and emotions with those thoughts as you open yourself to knowing God and hearing him;

   c. be open to how the Holy Spirit might want you to apply these meditations to your life. You engage your WILL, desire, and determination in response to the Holy Spirit giving you an idea of how you might resolve to do something or avoid something based on your meditation.

7.   Allow a few minutes to close in prayer. Thank God for how he spoke to you. Then pray aloud together the following Catholic "Prayer after Meditation."

I thank you, my God, for the good resolutions, affections and inspirations that you have given to me in this time of prayer. I beg your help in putting them into effect. My Immaculate Mother, Saint Joseph my father, and my guardian angel, intercede for me.

Amen.

Psalm 103

[1] Bless the Lord, O my soul,
  and all that is within me,
  bless his holy name.
[2] Bless the Lord, O my soul,
  and do not forget all his benefits—
[3] who forgives all your iniquity,
  who heals all your diseases,
[4] who redeems your life from the Pit,
  who crowns you with steadfast love and mercy,
[5] who satisfies you with good as long as you live
  so that your youth is renewed like the eagle's.

[6] The Lord works vindication
  and justice for all who are oppressed.
[7] He made known his ways to Moses,
  his acts to the people of Israel.
[8] The Lord is merciful and gracious,
  slow to anger and abounding in steadfast love.
[9] He will not always accuse,
  nor will he keep his anger for ever.
[10] He does not deal with us according to our sins,
  nor repay us according to our iniquities.
[11] For as the heavens are high above the earth,

so great is his steadfast love towards those who fear him;
12 as far as the east is from the west,
  so far he removes our transgressions from us.
13 As a father has compassion for his children,
  so the Lord has compassion for those who fear him.
14 For he knows how we were made;
  he remembers that we are dust.

15 As for mortals, their days are like grass;
  they flourish like a flower of the field;
16 for the wind passes over it, and it is gone,
  and its place knows it no more.
17 But the steadfast love of the Lord is from everlasting to everlasting
  on those who fear him,
  and his righteousness to children's children,
18 to those who keep his covenant
  and remember to do his commandments.

19 The Lord has established his throne in the heavens,
  and his kingdom rules over all.
20 Bless the Lord, O you his angels,
  you mighty ones who do his bidding,
  obedient to his spoken word.
21 Bless the Lord, all his hosts,
  his ministers that do his will.
22 Bless the Lord, all his works,
  in all places of his dominion.
Bless the Lord, O my soul.

Planning Daily Prayer

Leader: Go through the questions below with your discipleship partner. They will help him/ her come up with a solid plan for their first week of prayer. Mornings are considered the ideal time for prayer because the hustle and bustle of the day hasn't yet begun so the mind is less "busy." (Jesus rose in the morning while it was still very dark.) Morning does not work for everyone. They should seek a time when they are typically free. Ideally, the discipleship partner sets a time that works daily but often students open hours vary from day to day.

Most important is for you to help your discipleship partner think creatively by sensitively and helpfully asking questions and/or making suggestions. Sometimes the only window of time to pray on a given day falls between his/her classes. In that case a study carol in the library or some similarly quiet spot can work well.

Various tools can help with prayer. A quiet place is essential. The campus chapel often works better than a dorm room. Encourage your discipleship partner to use a journal for prayer if that helps them focus. Some people hold a cross or rosary as an aid to focusing.

Check out Appendix E for Week 5 ahead of time to look at the list of suggested books of the Bible and devotional reading. Think of your own suggestions. When you get to question 3 turn to the appendix with them and talk through possibilities. Encourage them to meditate on Scripture at least half of the time. Encourage them to also choose a good spiritual book to integrate. Tell them about the local Catholic or Christian bookstore; you might consider planning a time to go together. You can email them book suggestions and where to buy them online. You might consider lending them a devotional book to check out before they buy it. This is a good time to give them the packet of daily readings for Mass that you printed out for them.

Gently exhort them to treat their prayer time like an appointment that they can't cancel. Planning all the aids and reading in the world won't make a whit of difference unless the disciple actually commits to a time and keeps that commitment.

They are going to feel the sacrifice of this time in their lives so be encouraging. Tell them you will be praying for them this week and suggest they pray for themselves – that God would strengthen their firm resolution when tested. Remind them to trust in God's gentleness with us. Assure them that praying for the desire to pray is itself a prayer God rejoices to hear. Model the importance of this by making such a prayer part of your closing prayer for yourself and for him/her.

1. **What time each day can you carve out twenty to thirty minutes for prayer? When is the best time of day for you? Are you a night person or a morning person? How can you give your best to God while also working within the limits and demands of your daily schedule?**

2. Where is the best place for you to pray? What does your state in life allow? Do you pray best at home, outside, or is it better for you to stop by a chapel? Do you walk, drive or bike by a chapel on the way home from work?

3. What material do you want to use for your meditation time? Do you have a Bible? Is there a gospel or letter from the Bible that has piqued your interest? Would you like to follow the daily readings of the Church? Is there a spiritual book or saint you would like to read? Please see Appendix E for a list of suggestions.

4. Take a few minutes right now to think through and write down where and when you can commit to praying every day. Add this time to your daily planner!

	Sunday	Monday	Tuesday	Wednesday	Thursday	Friday	Saturday
When / how long							
Where							

Closing Prayer

Devotion to Scripture

Week 6

"This book of the law shall not depart out of your mouth,
but you shall meditate on it day and night . . .
for then you shall make your way prosperous,
and then you shall have good success."

Joshua 1:8

Opening Prayer

Introduction

1. How did prayer go this week? Were you able to stick with the times and places you had chosen to pray?

Leader: Asking each week about the discipleship partner's prayer life keeps him/her accountable, but be careful never to sound disapproving or judgmental when he/she hasn't achieved his/her goals. This is almost inevitable. Prayer in the earliest stages is a struggle. Affirm the efforts they did make. Express understanding about the ways our good intentions go astray and recognize that developing a disciplined prayer life is challenging. Share the fruits of perseverance in prayer you have known as a possible motivational tool. If they did pray on a few days, ask whether he/she noticed any differences in those days from others.

2. Was there ever a time in your life when a particular Scripture passage became important to you for some reason? Or does any story from Scripture stand out as one you particularly like?

Leader: The discipleship partner may stare at you blankly and answer "no." In that case, move rapidly to the Wheel. Sometime a person searches her mind for any passages she can remember. Your questions can help her articulate why God might have brought that passage to mind in that moment, for example, "What do you particularly like or dislike about that passage?" This question demonstrates to your discipleship partner both that he/she already has some Scripture stories that have imbedded in his/her heart, or that God can speak in an instant when we turn our minds to the Scripture.

The Wheel

1. Why do you think prayer and word are on the vertical axis?

*Leader: Make sure your discipleship partner comes to understand that prayer and word are the means by which we have a **relationship** with Jesus, and so with all persons of the Trinity. (Vertical/up and down indicates our connection to heaven.)*

2.   What is necessary for any relationship?

Leader: Communication - All real relationship is dialogical: talking and listening. In prayer, we both talk and listen. We hear the Word of God in the Scriptures.

Scripture for Memorization

2 Timothy 3:16
"All Scripture is inspired by God and profitable for teaching, for reproof, for correction, and for training in righteousness…"

Joshua 1:8
"This book of the law shall not depart out of your mouth, but you shall meditate on it day and night, that you may be careful to do according to all that is written in it; for then you shall make your way prosperous, and then you shall have good success."

Reading

"Dogmatic Constitution on Divine Revelation" (Dei Verbum)

…The sacred synod also earnestly and especially urges all the Christian faithful…, to learn by frequent reading of the divine Scriptures the "excellent knowledge of Jesus Christ" (Phil. 3:8). "For ignorance of the Scriptures is ignorance of Christ."(St. Jerome) Therefore, they should gladly put themselves in touch with the sacred text itself… And let them remember that prayer should accompany the reading of Sacred Scripture, so that God and man may talk together; for "we speak to Him when we pray; we hear Him when we read the divine saying." (St. Ambrose)[1]

1.   Did you know of the bishops' exhortation at Vatican II "to learn by frequent reading of the divine Scriptures the 'excellent knowledge of Jesus Christ'?"

2.   What does it mean to you that they made this exhortation?

[1] "Dogmatic Constitution on Divine Revelation" (*Dei Verbum*), Chapter 3, paragraph 25, Documents of Vatican II.

Pope Benedict XVI

Bible-reading is placed at the centre of Christian life, which gives to Catholic piety a new orientation. The prayer life of the Catholic Christian hitherto, apart from participating in the divine liturgy, had been determined chiefly by the various forms of devotion – rosary, stations of the cross, veneration of the Sacred Heart, etc. – which had arisen since the late middle ages and during more recent times. Private reading of Scripture played no important role and even for meditation and for preaching was not considered of prime importance. It may thus be regarded as an event of special importance for the development of the spiritual life when our text (*Dei Verbum*) gives a special place to the personal acquaintance with Scripture as a fundamental form of the relation to God and emphasizes its importance with the emphatic utterance of St. Jerome "for ignorance of the Scriptures is ignorance of Christ". It is important to see that the Council is not here concerned with intellectual or informative knowledge of Scripture, or one that is motivated by cultural or educational considerations, but it means the reading of the Bible as prayer, as entering into that dialogue with the Lord, for the living realization of which in faith, in prayer the pages of Scripture, are, as it were, waiting. It is fair to say that Catholic piety has still largely to discover the Bible properly... [2]

1. **What do you think this commentary on Dei Verbum means when it says the Church now gives a special place to reading the Scriptures "as a fundamental form of the relation to God?"**

*Leader: This is slightly complicated language. You may have to help them realize that all communication has a form. The director of the mentoring program communicates with you, the mentor, here in the form of written language. You often communicate with friends and family in the form of oral conversation, or electronic written conversation with instant messaging. What does it mean to say that reading Scripture is a fundamental **form** of a relationship with God?*

2. **Have you read Scripture as prayer, a means for God to communicate with you, and build your relationship?**

[2] "Dogmatic Constitution on Divine Revelation," <u>Commentary on Documents of Vatican II, Volume III</u>, written by Joseph Ratzinger, now Pope Benedict XVI pages 270-271

Mark 6:7-13, 30-52

Leader: The following Scripture reading and questions are meant to help your discipleship partner "discover the Bible properly" by learning to pray with Scripture. There are many ways to pray with Scripture. This section from Mark is to be read as a "prayer of consideration," to use the description of St. Ignatius of Loyola his classic, The Spiritual Exercises of Ignatius Loyola. This is one of the most fruitful ways for us to pray with Scripture because it uses our reason, a faculty students are very much in the habit of exercising. Considering text comes naturally, but learning to hear God in that consideration takes practice. Your goal is to help them have this experience so they can later practice it on their own.

When we engage the stories and teachings of Scripture with the intellect God can plant ideas in our reason and imagination. We don't always need to be in a heightened contemplative state for God to work in us with Scripture. God uses all our faculties to communicate with us.

Joseph Tetlow, S.J., who has translated Ignatius' Spiritual Exercises for modern times (The 19th Annotation), writes of the prayer of consideration: "This is what Jesus of Nazareth urged his disciples to do when he invited them to 'consider the lilies of the field.' He was not asking them to puzzle out some botanical conundrum about lilies. He was asking them to turn their minds to the simple facts about the little red flowers growing in the stony field and to let their hearts grasp what flowers and fields told them about the love of God their Creator and Lord... Consideration is a readily available way of praying continuously, an almost intrinsic activity..." (Joseph Tetlow, Making Choices in Christ: The Foundations of Ignatian Spirituality).

This section of Mark's gospel is useful for exploring how the early followers of Jesus responded, or might have responded, to the situations they encountered while following Jesus – a useful consideration for someone seeking to grow as a disciple.

The questions appear in both your booklets. Tell your discipleship partner that you will both take ten to fifteen minutes to read the passage and go through the questions individually. Encourage him/her to underline anything of interest in his or her Bible or in the booklet, and to jot down his/her answers on a separate piece of paper.

This exercise can be done in the same room, even at the same table if you're in a coffee shop. Just agree to work alone for a time, and be sensitive to when your discipleship partner seems to have completed the reading and questions. Come back together for discussion. Some of this might be intellectual awareness, such as "I never realized that Jesus walked on water right after the multiplication of the loaves…" You would then want to ask why that is significant to him/her. Concentrate conversation on realizations that could pertain to your discipleship partner's spiritual life. For example, if your partner says that he/she liked thinking about how the apostles might have had failures they didn't report to Jesus, explore what your discipleship partner feels he/she can and can't take to Jesus…

Demonstrate how to prepare to read Scripture by beginning with a prayer for divine assistance, such as: "Dear Lord, help us to hear your voice in a new way this day, through this reading of your holy Word. Open our hearts Lord. We love you and want to know you more. We long to learn to follow you, Lord. Use those saints who followed you when you walked the earth to teach us now. Amen." Use words natural to your own spirituality.

Many different issues could be pursued in this long section from Mark. These questions are designed to help you and your discipleship partner consider life as a disciple. If another train of questioning takes over, that could be the Holy Spirit. Feel free to pursue it, but strive to demonstrate in your conversation that God can speak to us through applying our reason and imagination to Scripture.

[7] And he called to him the twelve, and began to send them out two by two, and gave them authority over the unclean spirits. [8] He charged them to take nothing for their journey except a staff; no bread, no bag, no money in their belts; [9] but to wear sandals and not put on two tunics. [10] And he said to them, "Where you enter a house, stay there until you leave the place. [11] And if any place will not receive you and they refuse to hear you, when you leave, shake off the dust that is on your feet for a testimony against them." [12] So they went out and preached that men should repent. [13] And they cast out many demons, and anointed with oil many that were sick and healed them… [30] The apostles returned to Jesus, and told him all that they had done and taught. [31] And he said to them, "Come away by yourselves to a lonely place, and rest a while." For many were coming and going, and they had no leisure even to eat. [32] And they went away in the boat to a lonely place by themselves. [33] Now many saw them going, and knew them, and they ran there on foot from all the towns, and got there ahead of them. [34] As he went ashore he saw a great throng, and he had compassion on them, because they were like sheep without a shepherd; and he began to teach them many things. [35] And when it grew late, his disciples came to him and said, "This is a lonely place, and the hour is now late; [36] send

them away, to go into the country and villages round about and buy themselves something to eat." [37] But he answered them, "You give them something to eat." And they said to him, "Shall we go and buy two hundred denarii worth of bread, and give it to them to eat?" [38] And he said to them, "How many loaves have you? Go and see." And when they had found out, they said, "Five, and two fish." [39] Then he commanded them all to sit down by companies upon the green grass. [40] So they sat down in groups, by hundreds and by fifties. [41] And taking the five loaves and the two fish he looked up to heaven, and blessed, and broke the loaves, and gave them to the disciples to set before the people; and he divided the two fish among them all. [42] And they all ate and were satisfied. [43] And they took up twelve baskets full of broken pieces and of the fish. [44] And those who ate the loaves were five thousand men. [45] Immediately he made his disciples get into the boat and go before him to the other side, to Beth-saida, while he dismissed the crowd. [46] And after he had taken leave of them, he went up on the mountain to pray. [47] And when evening came, the boat was out on the sea, and he was alone on the land. [48] And he saw that they were making headway painfully, for the wind was against them. And about the fourth watch of the night he came to them, walking on the sea. He meant to pass by them, [49] but when they saw him walking on the sea they thought it was a ghost, and cried out; [50] for they all saw him, and were terrified. But immediately he spoke to them and said, "Take heart, it is I; have no fear." [51] And he got into the boat with them and the wind ceased. And they were utterly astounded, [52] for they did not understand about the loaves, but their hearts were hardened.

1. How do you think the apostles felt about not carrying food, water, money or a change of clothes?

2. What does dust do when it is stuck to your sandal? Why would it be important to shake it off physically? How does that translate to the rejection of the work of healing, preaching repentance and casting out evil spirits?

3. The apostles returned and told Jesus about their successes; do you think they also experienced failures?

4. What do you think is Jesus' motivation in calling them away to rest at a quiet place without other people?

5. How do you think they felt when the arrived to find crowds waiting for them?

How do you think they felt when Jesus started teaching those crowds?

6. What do you think was the apostles' motivation in asking Jesus to send the people away?

7. How do you think they felt when he said, "You give them something to eat!"

8. Why do you think Jesus sent the apostles ahead of him in the boat? How do you think the apostles felt about it?

9. How might the apostles have felt rowing against the strong wind?

10. Why do you think Jesus "meant to pass them by?"

11. What effect does Jesus have on the apostles and disciples?

12. Do you ever feel frightened by Jesus?

13. What do you think Mark means by: "their hearts were hardened?" How does a hardened heart keep us from apprehending what is before us?

Leader: The following passages in italics are cumbersome for discussion, but may be helpful for you to know as a mentor. Familiarize yourself with this doctrine on Scripture in case questions arise.

Dogmatic Constitution on Divine Revelation (Dei Verbum), Chapter 2, portion of paragraph 10, <u>Documents of Vatican II</u>.

> *Sacred tradition and Sacred Scripture form one sacred deposit of the Word of God, committed to the Church… But the task of authentically interpreting the Word of God, whether written or handed on, has been entrusted exclusively to the living teaching office of the Church, whose authority is exercised in the name of Jesus Christ. This teaching office is not above the Word of God, but serves it, teaching only what has been handed on, listening to it devoutly, guarding it scrupulously and explaining it faithfully in accord with a divine commission and with the help of the Holy Spirit, it draws from this one deposit of faith everything which it presents for belief as divinely revealed.*

Some Catholics misunderstand the relationship of Catholicism to Scripture. When controversy arises, the magisterium reserves the right to ultimate interpretation, but the magisterium also subjects itself to Scripture. "This teaching office is not above the Word of God, but serves it…"

Chapter II, portions of paragraph 11

Those divinely revealed realities which are contained and presented in Sacred Scripture have been committed to writing under the inspiration of the Holy Spirit. For holy mother Church, relying on the belief of the Apostles (see John 20:31; 2 Tim. 3:16; 2 Peter 1:19-20, 3:15-16), holds that the books of both the Old and New Testaments in their entirety, with all their parts, are sacred and canonical because written under the inspiration of the Holy Spirit, they have God as their author and have been handed on as such to the Church herself…

Therefore, since everything asserted by the inspired authors or sacred writers must be held to be asserted by the Holy Spirit, it follows that the books of Scripture must be acknowledged as teaching solidly, faithfully and without error that truth which God wanted put into sacred writings **for the sake of salvation.** *Therefore 'all Scripture is divinely inspired and has its use for teaching the truth and refuting error, for reformation of manners and discipline in right living, so that the man who belongs to God may be efficient and equipped for good work of every kind' (2 Tim. 3:16-17, Greek text).*

The concept of inspiration is often connected with inerrancy. In the first paragraph the Church certifies that the Bible, taken as a whole, is a reliable witness to God's revelation as communicated in the formative period. It is inerrant in the sense the writers were prevented from falsifying what God had revealed.

Some Christians teach that every word of the Bible is literally inerrant. Catholics teach that that which is necessary "for the sake of salvation" is inerrant. This statement is carefully crafted to affirm the value of the Bible as a whole for transmitting in its purity the truth that leads to salvation, but it leaves open the possibility that individual authors may have erred especially with regard to scientific and historical matters not connected with salvation.

This does not mean that the Bible is a patchwork of errant and inerrant passages. The whole Bible is authoritative in what it affirms about the revelation of God and the plan of salvation. Individual passages must be interpreted according to the intentions of the authors *and in their historical and literary context. Vatican II did not favor a fundamentalist literalism in which each sentence, taken in itself, can be considered absolute.*

Conclusion

Leader: Like anything, we all feel attracted to spiritual things to different degrees. Just as we need to ask God to give us the desire to pray, so also we rely on him to give us the desire to want to know Christ through Scripture. When we find that we lack a certain spiritual appetite, we should not let discouragement rule the day, but rather be honest with God about this lack and ask him to make us more open ; to dispose us to receive the gift of desire for Scripture that he wants to give us. After discussing the personal reflection questions below, you may want to include in the closing prayer a petition for yourself and your discipleship partner, something such as: "For the blessing of conversing with God through Scripture, that you might truly know in your heart and through experience of God speaking to you through his Word.

1. **How might you integrate Scripture into your spiritual diet? Will Scripture be part of the materials you use during your daily prayer?**

2. **What did you think of Ignatius' "prayer of consideration" that we did today? Did it help you to get to know Christ, or something about being his disciple? If yes, how?**

Closing Prayer

Our Salvation in Community
week 7

*"For where two or three are gathered in my name,
there am I in the midst of them."*

Matthew 18:20

Opening Prayer

Introduction

1. How did prayer go this week? Were you able to stick with the times and places you had chosen to pray? Any particular gifts, consolations or challenges?

2. Do you have friends with whom you share an intense interest such as playing a sport or pursuing a hobby?

3. What is the gift of those particular relationships?

4. What is your relationship with those people compared to your relationships with others who do not share this interest?

The Wheel

Leader: Convey the following in your own words.

Community is on the horizontal axis because it indicates our earthly activity, (as opposed to connection to heaven, like prayer and the Word on the vertical.) The communal spoke represents our need to be in loving relationship with other members of the body of Christ, to encourage and to be encouraged by them. (See Hebrews 10:24-25 in Scripture for Memorization section.) We are social by nature – that is the way God made us. No one is an isolated individual: we all have parents and often siblings. If we do not because of death or alienation, the need of our hearts drives us to seek out these kinds of familial relationships.

Scripture for Memorization

Heb 10:24-25

"And let us consider how to stir up one another to love and good works, not neglecting to meet together, as is the habit of some, but encouraging one another, and all the more as you see the Day drawing near."

Matthew 18:20

"For where two or three are gathered in my name, there am I in the midst of them."

Reading

Luke 15:11-32

Leader: Many themes could be explored in this well known story. Without crushing anything about conversion, the loving forgiveness of God, or anything else, you will want to focus this discussion as much as possible along the lines of the questions provided in order to consider the role of community in our spiritual life.

[11] And he said, "There was a man who had two sons; [12] and the younger of them said to his father, 'Father, give me the share of property that falls to me.' And he divided his living between them. [13] Not many days later, the younger son gathered all he had and took his journey into a far country, and there he squandered his property in loose living. [14] And when he had spent everything, a great famine arose in that country, and he began to be in want. [15] So he went and joined himself to one of the citizens of that country, who sent him into his fields to feed swine. [16] And he would gladly have fed on the pods that the swine ate; and no one gave him anything. [17] But when he came to himself he said, 'How many of my father's hired servants have bread enough and to spare, but I perish here with hunger! [18] I will arise and go to my father, and I will say to him, "Father, I have sinned against heaven and before you; [19] I am no longer worthy to be called your son; treat me as one of your hired servants."' [20] And he arose and came to his father. But while he was yet at a distance, his father saw him and had compassion, and ran and embraced him and kissed him. [21] And the son said to him, 'Father, I have sinned against heaven and before you; I am no longer worthy to be called your son.' [22] But the father said to his servants, 'Bring quickly the best robe, and put it on him; and put a ring on his hand, and shoes on his feet; [23] and bring the fatted calf and kill it, and let us eat and make merry; [24] for this my son was dead, and is alive again; he was lost, and is found.' And they began to make merry. [25] "Now his elder son was in the field; and as he came and drew near to the house, he heard music and dancing. [26] And he called one of the servants and asked what this meant. [27] And he said to him, 'Your brother has come, and your father has killed the fatted calf, because he has received him safe and sound.' [28] But he was angry and refused to go in. His father came out and entreated him, [29] but he answered his father, 'Lo,

these many years I have served you, and I never disobeyed your command; yet you never gave me a kid, that I might make merry with my friends. [30] But when this son of yours came, who has devoured your living with harlots, you killed for him the fatted calf!' 31 And he said to him, 'Son, you are always with me, and all that is mine is yours. 32 It was fitting to make merry and be glad, for this your brother was dead, and is alive; he was lost, and is found.'"

1. What might have been the attitude of the prodigal son to his relatives and community at home in order for him to move so far away from them, physically and spiritually?

2. What would you guess his relationships were like in the land where he squandered his wealth? What kind of relationships develop when someone is spending money fast and frivolously?

3. What do you think his relationships with others at the pig farm might have been like? (Jews and Muslims have no contact with pigs because they are considered unclean.)

4. What happens when the prodigal son comes home?

5. How do you think the prodigal son felt about his brother's disapproval?

6. After the party with the fatted-calf is over and the prodigal son has settled into life at home, what might his relationships be like with his Father, brothers, servants?

7. Have you ever moved or traveled far from family and friends? Did you face different temptations than you did when in community? If you haven't yet done this, what kind of temptations do you think a person encounters at such a time?

St. Teresa of Avila

Now I realize what a danger it is at an age when one should begin to cultivate the virtues to associate with people who do not know the vanity of the world but are rather getting ready to throw themselves into it....

So it happened with me. I imitated all that was harmful... It frightens me to think of the harm a bad companion can do and if I hadn't experienced it, I wouldn't believe it... From such experience I understand the profit that comes from good companionship. And I am certain that if at that age I had gone around with virtuous persons, I would have remained whole in virtue. For should I have had when that age someone to teach me to fear God, my soul would have gained strength, not fallen[1]

1. Have you had an experience such as St. Teresa's where a friend led you astray?

2. What do you think is "the profit that comes from good companionship?" How have you benefitted from being part of a strong Christian community? Do you have that in your life right now? How might you go about finding it?

Acts 2:42-47

[42] And they devoted themselves to the apostles' teaching and fellowship, to the breaking of bread and the prayers. [43] And fear came upon every soul; and many wonders and signs were done through the apostles. [44] And all who believed were together and had all things in common; [45] and they sold their possessions and goods and distributed them to all, as any had need. [46] And day by day, attending the temple together and breaking bread in their homes, they partook of food with glad and generous hearts, [47] praising God and having favor with all the people. And the Lord added to their number day by day those who were being saved.

1. What are the features of the early Christian community?

2. How does the community those early Christians experienced compare with the community you experience?

3. Do you think that type of community is people's common experience of Church?

4. What hinders such Christian community? How could we overcome these hindrances?

5. The disciples gather daily to break bread as Jesus taught them. What do you think this means for us?

---

[1] Teresa of Avila: The Book of her Life – translated by Kieran Kavanaugh, O.C.D. and Otilio Rodriguez, O.C.D., pages 35-6

Leaders: You will want to use the last question as an opportunity to talk about the importance of Sunday Mass, and the gift of daily Mass.

6.   How do we go about devoting ourselves to the apostles' instructions?

Leader: Make sure your discipleship partner realizes that they devote themselves to these instructions both through listening to the heirs of the apostles through apostolic succession, the bishops, and listening to the original apostles through exactly what you're doing: Scripture study. Attending carefully to the readings at Mass is another way Catholics listen to the original apostles.

Closing Prayer

Leader: Be sure to include in your prayer a request that God lead us to friends and associates who love Christ and want to serve him. Ask God to break down any barriers within us that prevent our participation in real Christian fellowship. If this is an issue for your discipleship partner, you might also pray for Gods help to lovingly withdraw from any companions who lead us away from the virtues and into vice.

Evangelization

Week 8

"For I am not ashamed of the gospel:
it is the power of God for salvation
to every one who has faith…"

Romans 1:16

Opening Prayer

Introduction

1. How did your prayer go this week?

2. Consider life "after the party" for the prodigal son: How do you think he would feel if after his return home a friend started scheming to claim his inheritance early? Suppose this friend shared his plan to run off where he could live free from the constraints of family and community. What do you think he would say to that friend?

3. How do you think he would feel if his friends took for granted the love of their parents, or didn't believe in God?

4. What do you think the prodigal son would do in those circumstances, given his experience?

5. Have you or has anyone you have known well separated themselves from the community of the church? How did you feel about that?

Leader: These questions should help your discipleship partner realize that a transformed life is the source of our desire for all to live in the community of Christ's love. This is important because often people don't realize the negative associations they have of evangelization. They think of it as proselytizing: rude, pushy people in your face about what should concern only themselves. The Scripture on the Woman at the Well provides a contrasting example to these negative stereotypes.

The Wheel

Leader: Please put this in your own words as you examine the Wheel. Like community, evangelization is on the horizontal axis because it concerns our life on earth and our relationship with our Christian community and others. People who recognize their lives as transformed through the love of Christ naturally witness to good news joyously by how they live, what they say, and how a community of love sustains them and challenges them. These three evangelistic expressions are traditionally called witnessing through word, life, and community (also referred to as 3-D witnessing). When we follow Jesus closely we want to share with others the joy, peace, and love we have found in Him. It becomes an irresistible overflow of our life in, with and through Christ.

Be aware of timing as you launch into the passage below. Your discussion will be rich because the passage is! Be sure to leave enough time for the application questions at the end. You want your discipleship partner to leave this session having applied the concepts in John 4 to his/her life. They should feel encouraged and inspired to open themselves more to the Holy Spirit's promptings to witness to people they know.

Scripture for Memorization

Matthew 4:19
"And he (Jesus) said to them, 'Follow me, and I will make you fishers of men.'"

Romans 1:16
"For I am not ashamed of the gospel: it is the power of God for salvation to every one who has faith, to the Jew first and also to the Greek."

Reading

John 4: 3-43

³ [Jesus] left Judea and departed again to Galilee. ⁴ He had to pass through Samaria. ⁵ So he came to a city of Samaria, called Sychar, near the field that Jacob gave to his son Joseph. ⁶ Jacob's well was there, and so Jesus, wearied as he was with his journey, sat down beside the well. It was about the sixth hour. ⁷ There came a woman of Samaria to draw water. Jesus said to her, "Give me a drink." ⁸ For his disciples had gone away into the city to buy food. ⁹ The Samaritan woman said to him, "How is it that you, a Jew, ask a drink of me, a woman of Samaria?" For Jews have no dealings with Samaritans. ¹⁰ Jesus answered her, "If you knew the gift of God, and who it is that is saying to you, 'Give me a drink,' you would have asked him, and he would have given you living water." ¹¹ The woman said to him, "Sir, you have nothing to draw with, and the well is deep; where do you get that living water? ¹² Are you greater than our father Jacob, who gave us the well, and drank from it himself, and his sons, and his cattle?" ¹³ Jesus said to her, "Every one who drinks of this water will thirst again, ¹⁴ but whoever drinks of the water that I shall give him will never thirst; the water that I shall give him will become in him

a spring of water welling up to eternal life." [15] The woman said to him, "Sir, give me this water, that I may not thirst, nor come here to draw." [16] Jesus said to her, "Go, call your husband, and come here." [17] The woman answered him, "I have no husband." Jesus said to her, "You are right in saying, 'I have no husband'; [18] for you have had five husbands, and he whom you now have is not your husband; this you said truly." [19] The woman said to him, "Sir, I perceive that you are a prophet. [20] Our fathers worshiped on this mountain; and you say that in Jerusalem is the place where men ought to worship." [21] Jesus said to her, "Woman, believe me, the hour is coming when neither on this mountain nor in Jerusalem will you worship the Father. [22] You worship what you do not know; we worship what we know, for salvation is from the Jews. [23] But the hour is coming, and now is, when the true worshipers will worship the Father in spirit and truth, for such the Father seeks to worship him. [24] God is spirit, and those who worship him must worship in spirit and truth." [25] The woman said to him, "I know that Messiah is coming (he who is called Christ); when he comes, he will show us all things." [26] Jesus said to her, "I who speak to you am he." [27] Just then his disciples came. They marveled that he was talking with a woman, but none said, "What do you wish?" or, "Why are you talking with her?" [28] So the woman left her water jar, and went away into the city, and said to the people, [29] "Come, see a man who told me all that I ever did. Can this be the Christ?" [30] They went out of the city and were coming to him. [31] Meanwhile the disciples besought him, saying, "Rabbi, eat." [32] But he said to them, "I have food to eat of which you do not know." [33] So the disciples said to one another, "Has any one brought him food?" [34] Jesus said to them, "My food is to do the will of him who sent me, and to accomplish his work. [35] Do you not say, 'There are yet four months, then comes the harvest? I tell you, lift up your eyes, and see how the fields are already white for harvest. [36] He who reaps receives wages, and gathers fruit for eternal life, so that sower and reaper may rejoice together. [37] For here the saying holds true, 'One sows and another reaps.' [38] I sent you to reap that for which you did not labor; others have labored, and you have entered into their labor." [39] Many Samaritans from that city believed in him because of the woman's testimony, "He told me all that I ever did." [40] So when the Samaritans came to him, they asked him to stay with them; and he stayed there two days. [41] And many more believed because of his word. [42] They said to the woman, "It is no longer because of your words that we believe, for we have heard for ourselves, and we know that this is indeed the Savior of the world." [43] After the two days he departed to Galilee.

Leader: Things to know and tell your discipleship partner about Samaria and inhabitants as you ask the questions:

- *The typical Jewish path north went around Samaria which was considered lawless and dangerous.*

- *The Samaritans were held in contempt by Jews. They considered Samarians religious apostates who had mixed the purity of Israel's worship with idolatry. (Most biblical historians and archeologists believe this religious syncretism occurred after the invasion of the northern Kingdom of Israel by the Assyrians.) Many biblical scholars also believe that Samaritan worship on Mt. Gerazim predated the priestly movement in Judea and the commands in Hebrew Scriptures to worship only in Jerusalem.*

- *Jewish custom dictated that Jesus not talk to the woman at the well because:*
  - *Jewish men weren't allowed to talk to any unknown women.*
  - *Jews had nothing to do with Samaritans.*
  - *She came to draw water at noon, the hottest time of the day in a very hot climate. Many biblical scholars believe she must have sought to avoid the cooler morning times when the other women characteristically drew water.*

1. **How do you think the disciples felt as they were passing through Samaria, an area Jews generally avoided?**

2. **What is Jesus' situation when he approaches the woman? What does he want?**

3. **Does Jesus really need this woman to give him a drink of water? What might be his motivation in asking?**

4. **In verses 10-14, Jesus offers her a drink. What contrasts does Jesus make between the water from his well and that from Jacob's well? What does this reveal about him and his purpose?**

Leader: you might want to make a list with two columns for comparison.

Some points that your conversations should consider.

- *Jacob's well was for his sons and his flocks, Jesus' well is for everyone.*
- *Jacob's well temporarily satisfies bodily thirst, Jesus' living water satisfies greater needs.*
- *She labors; Jesus offers a drink that overflows super-abundantly.*
- *Jacob's well is man-made, Jesus' well is a God-given spring.*
- *Jesus wants to satisfy our real needs forever.*

5. **In verse 19 ff., why does the woman suddenly change the subject and begin talking about the controversy over the proper place to worship?**

    - *Perhaps, she wants to deflect Jesus' attention from her issue, the fact that she is in great need of living water.*
    - *Perhaps, she is testing him to see if he is going to reject her the way that the other Jews have for not worshipping in the right place. Is Jesus a prophet for her?*
    - *Perhaps, having realized that Jesus is a prophet, she is prompted to tell him that she understands the differences between Jews and Samaritans.*
    - *Perhaps she is taking the focus off of herself and putting it back on to Jesus to avoid deeper exploration of her life. She isn't defensive. Instead, she wants to know more about this amazing man.*

6. **When the woman finds out that Jesus already knows about her many relationships and yet has still spoken to her as a person, how might this have made her feel?**

7. **Instead of allowing her to deflect his comments, how does Jesus offer her hope (vv. 21-24)?**

    - *He tells her that she is worried about the wrong concerns.*
    - *The mode of worship is now to be in spirit and in truth, which transcends all ethnic, gender and local considerations.*

8. **How did being known through and through by Jesus, faults and all, affect the Samaritan woman?**

9. **What is the significance of Jesus revealing his identity first to this woman (in John's gospel)?**

10. How do the disciples feel when they returned to see Jesus talking to the Samaritan woman?

11. Jesus' friends are disturbed because Jesus is breaking a cultural taboo by speaking with an unknown woman. Why would Jesus do this?

12. How is this conversation with Jesus good news for the woman? What about the conversation do you think leads her to believe and witness?

13. What seems to be the emphasis of the woman's testimony to the people (v. 28-29)?

14. What is compelling about: "He told me everything I've ever done?" How would her life situation influence how she chose to witness?

15. What are the effects of her testimony (vv. 30, 39-42)?

16. After his encounter with the Samaritan woman, what does Jesus want to teach his disciples (vv. 31-38)?

17. Trace what the characters wanted, what they ultimately received, and how they received it. You may want to write this on a piece of paper. Touch on the Samaritan woman, the disciples, the villagers and Jesus.

Leader: After you and your discipleship partner have written responses for and discussed question 17, please turn to the Appendix F for Week 8 to read and discuss considerations for question 17.

18. Have you ever shared your testimony or faith story with anyone, whether formally or informally? What was that like for you? What made you do it? How did the person(s) respond?

19. The following quote is from On Evangelization in the Modern World, par 22 by Pope Paul VI, "Nevertheless, [the witness of life] always remains insufficient, because even the finest witness will prove ineffective in the long run if it is not explained, justified...and made explicit by a clear, unequivocal proclamation of the Lord Jesus. The Good News proclaimed by the witness of life sooner or later has to be proclaimed by the word of life."

- What opportunities do you have in your life to share Jesus?

- What challenges can this present?

- What ways can you grow as a witness of Christ?

- What relationships might the Holy Spirit be calling you to more intentionally cultivate? Are there people in your life that seem to be seeking God? Would they be open to going with you to an event or meeting such as a campus large group or a parish mission?

Leader: Your discipleship partner may never have shared his/her faith story before and may want training on how to do this. You may feel led to share with them how God has used your faith story when you have prepared it in the past. If the Holy Spirit leads, you could mentor them. Helpful materials can be found in the <u>Evangelical Catholic Ministry Handbook</u>, on the EC website (www.evangelicalcatholic.org), as well as at our weekend conferences and EC five day summer training camps. Invite the EC to come to your ministry to further train laity and staff for Catholic evangelization. We are his laborers and our fruitfulness depends on the Holy Spirit. We need to prepare for the harvest through trainings, conferences and through relationships that help to equip us.

Closing Prayer

Obedience to Christ and the Church

Week 9

*"Do not be conformed to this world,
but be transformed by the renewing of your minds,
so that you may discern what is the will of God –
what is good and acceptable and perfect."*

Romans 12:2

Opening Prayer

Introduction

1. Is there a time when you were disobedient to your parents?

2. Did that affect your relationship with them? If yes, how so?

3. If you were obedient to your parents most of the time, what were the positive affects of obedience for your relationship?

4. Why do you think God asks obedience of us?

The Wheel

Leader: Spend a few minutes discussing the Wheel. Obedience to God's ways and faithfulness to those things we ought to do for our salvation help keep us close to God's will. The placement of "obedience" around the rim of the Wheel illustrates this well. The spokes of the habits and aspects of discipleship emanate from the center, Christ and Christ experienced in the sacraments, but they end in nothing without the rim of obedience to connect them and carry the power of Christ into our lives and the world. Only obedience allows the Wheel to roll. If we are not obedient in living as disciples, then our Wheel isn't a wheel at all, but rather an incomplete, unstructured conglomeration of elements, some of which might be very good, but not as effective as they could be in a unified whole.

1. Draw the Wheel without the rim connecting to the spokes at areas where you are not able to obey the habits and aspects of discipleship. Then analyze how your Wheel would roll.

2. What does this say about the role of obedience in a disciple's life?

Scripture for Memorization

Romans 12:2
"Do not be conformed to this world, but be transformed by the renewing of your minds, so that you may discern what is the will of God -- what is good and acceptable and perfect."

John 14:21

"They who have my commandments and keep them are those who love me; and those who love me will be loved by my Father, and I will love them and reveal myself to them."

Reading

John 14: 20-21

"²⁰On that day you will know that I am in my Father, and you in me, and I in you. 21They who have my commandments and keep them are those who love me; and those who love me will be loved by my Father, and I will love them and reveal myself to them."

1. What can we learn about obedience from these verses?

2. Do you think there is a relationship between the spiritual union Jesus describes in verse 20 and the obedience he desires of us in verse 21? If yes, what relationship?

3. How would you describe the relationship between love and authority? Love and obedience?

4. How does a disciple find out what God desires and commands?

5. How can disobedience to Jesus' commands affect our relationship with Christ? …our relationship to others (the church)? Have you experienced a struggle like this? If yes would you feel comfortable sharing how? What did you learn from these experiences?

Catechism of the Catholic Church

Leader: Many people know that conscience is the final arbiter in Catholic thought. (Catechism of the Catholic Church 1790) But many, especially in the U.S. where the culture of individuality is so strong and unquestioned, think that this means the individual stands alone in splendid truth. This is decidedly NOT the church teachings. As paragraph 1790 of the Catechism of the Catholic Church states, "A human being must always obey the certain judgment of his conscience. If he were deliberately to act against it, he would condemn himself. Yet it can happen that moral conscience remains in ignorance and makes erroneous judgments…"

Conscience is not a fixed thing. It develops. It is our personal responsibility to work on that development. We do this by exploring church teachings in a truly open and teachable way, especially when we disagree. This exploration must be thorough – not just reading but talking to people whom we respect who accept and love the church's teaching. We must inform our reason so we can use it to explore the intellectual arguments both for and against our current belief.

Conscience is not just an inherent sense; it is a responsibility we can take lightly or seriously. If your disciple has concerns about church teaching - a not uncommon situation - explore with them how they might go about forming and informing their conscience on this topic. Real growth can come from honest questioning and responsible seeking. Telling people they just must accept church teaching is rarely fruitful, and can alienate people of good will.

Encourage people to be honest and diligent with the questions they have regarding various church teachings. People who "take little trouble to find out what is true and good" do not grow from their questions (Catechism of the Catholic Church 1791). Not only can they lead others astray by too much talking but they themselves are hindered by not taking responsibility to form their conscience and develop greater interiority (Catechism of the Catholic Church 1779).

> 1776 "Deep within his conscience man discovers a law which he has not laid upon himself but which he must obey. Its voice, ever calling him to love and to do what is good and to avoid evil, sounds in his heart at the right moment. . . . For man has in his heart a law inscribed by God. . . . His conscience is man's most secret core and his sanctuary. There he is alone with God whose voice echoes in his depths."[2]

> 1779 It is important for every person to be sufficiently present to himself in order to hear and follow the voice of his conscience. This requirement of *interiority* is all the more necessary as life often distracts us from any reflection, self-examination or introspection.

> > "Return to your conscience, question it. . . . Turn inward, brethren, and in everything you do, see God as your witness."[3]

[1]GS 16.
[2]GS 16.
[3]St. Augustine, In ep Jo. 8, 9: PL 35, 2041.

1783 Conscience must be informed and moral judgment enlightened... The education of conscience is indispensable for human beings who are subjected to negative influences and tempted by sin to prefer their own judgment and to reject authoritative teachings.

1784 The education of the conscience is a lifelong task. . . Prudent education teaches virtue; it prevents or cures fear, selfishness and pride, resentment arising from guilt, and feelings of complacency, born of human weakness and faults. The education of the conscience guarantees freedom and engenders peace of heart.

1785 In the formation of conscience the Word of God is the light for our path,[4] we must assimilate it in faith and prayer and put it into practice. We must also examine our conscience before the Lord's Cross. We are assisted by the gifts of the Holy Spirit, aided by the witness or advice of others and guided by the authoritative teaching of the Church.

1. **How does the <u>Catechism of the Catholic Church</u> define conscience? What is the relationship between conscience and obedience?**

2. **What can aid the disciple in actually hearing and following one's conscience? What can hinder one from hearing one's conscience?**

3. **What are the many ways a disciple forms his conscience?**

III. TO CHOOSE IN ACCORD WITH CONSCIENCE

1786 Faced with a moral choice, conscience can make either a right judgment in accordance with reason and the divine law or, on the contrary, an erroneous judgment that departs from them.

1787 Man is sometimes confronted by situations that make moral judgments less assured and decision difficult. But he must always seriously seek what is right and good and discern the will of God expressed in divine law.

1788 To this purpose, man strives to interpret the data of experience and the signs of the times assisted by the virtue of prudence, by the advice of competent people, and by the help of the Holy Spirit and his gifts.

[4]Cf. Ps 119:105.
[5]Cf. DH 14.

IV. ERRONEOUS JUDGMENT

1790 A human being must always obey the certain judgment of his conscience. If he were deliberately to act against it, he would condemn himself. Yet it can happen that moral conscience remains in ignorance and makes erroneous judgments about acts to be performed or already committed.

1791 This ignorance can often be imputed to personal responsibility. This is the case when a man "takes little trouble to find out what is true and good, or when conscience is by degrees almost blinded through the habit of committing sin."[6] In such cases, the person is culpable for the evil he commits.

1792 Ignorance of Christ and his Gospel, bad example given by others, enslavement to one's passions, assertion of a mistaken notion of autonomy of conscience, rejection of the Church's authority and her teaching, lack of conversion and of charity: these can be at the source of errors of judgment in moral conduct.

1793 If - on the contrary - the ignorance is invincible, or the moral subject is not responsible for his erroneous judgment, the evil committed by the person cannot be imputed to him. It remains no less an evil, a privation, a disorder. One must therefore work to correct the errors of moral conscience.

1. **On the one hand, the church teaches that human beings must obey the certain judgments of her conscience. Yet erroneous judgments are still made this way. How do you explain this? What does this say about the church's understanding of the human person?**

2. **What are the two types of ignorance described in the above paragraphs? How are they different?**

3. **What are some ways you can deepen the formation of your conscience? Do you have any specific areas of confusion or misunderstanding with regard to divine law and church teaching in which you need "to find out what is true and good?"**

Leader: A couple resources that might interest the discipleship partner with regard to forming his/her conscience:

[6]GS 16.

<u>Good News about Sex and Marriage</u> by Christopher West would answer almost any question on marriage and sexuality. It is in Q and A format. A chapter is easily copied from it. If you know that your discipleship partner has specific questions regarding the church's teachings on sexuality, make the effort to copy a chapter for them.

<u>Back to Virtue</u> by Peter Kreeft is an enjoyable read and a manageable introduction on living a virtuous, Christian life.

<u>Refutation of Moral Relativism: Interviews with an Absolutist</u> by Peter Kreeft

<u>The Truth about Homosexuality</u> by Fr. John Harvey addresses some of the arguments around genetic pre-disposition and in utero causal conditions. Harvey summarizes some research and theories of Christian doctors and therapists who understand homosexuality as a disorder, whether they use that Catholic terminology or not. Holds church's teaching as authoritative, but very concerned with the pastoral care of persons who experience same sex attraction. Fr. Harvey shares his vast knowledge of the topic. He founded and runs "Courage", a Catholic group for those who experience same sex attraction but accept the church's teaching.

Closing Prayer

Appendix A

For Week 2: Life in Christ – Being a Child of God

An Explanation of the Wheel

Wheel Illustration: The Basics of an Evangelical Catholic Spiritual Life

Illustrations over-simplify, but that is also their genius. Much easier for you to remember (and share) the contents of our little wheel, than that of a long, nuanced essay packed with references! The idea of this one here is that if you incorporate each of these elements into your life in Christ, your spiritual "wheel" will keep moving you closer to him.

The Hub: Christ

"I have been crucified with Christ; yet I live, no longer I, but Christ lives in me; insofar as I now live in the flesh, I live by faith in the Son of God who has loved me and given himself up for me" (Galatians 2:20).

In the hub of the Wheel, you find Christ, the one who made possible the healing, salvation, and redemption of our own life and of the human race. He is the God-man Jesus Christ, whose place in the center represents where He is in the place of human history, and where He should be in our life.

Inner Rim: Sacramental Life

"Whoever eats my flesh and drinks my blood remains in me and I in him" (John 6:56).

The sacramental life draws us ever more deeply into the life of Christ through his Body, the Church. Thus the sacramental life is drawn in a circle around Christ, the center of our life. We experience Jesus in a unique and powerful way when we receive one of these seven great gifts of the Church: Baptism, Eucharist, Confirmation, Reconciliation, Anointing of the Sick, Matrimony, and Holy Orders.

Outer Rim: Obedience

"Whoever has my commandments and observes them is the one who loves me. And whoever loves me will be loved by my Father, and I will love him and reveal myself to him" (John 14:21).

Obedience keeps it all together. God gives us the Scriptures and the Church to help us know how to follow him. It is definitely not always easy to live in obedience to his commandments, and sometimes it is extremely difficult, but God gives us his Holy Spirit who enables us to do all things in him. If you obey him even when it is difficult, he will work it out for your good as he promises in the Scriptures. Everything God has asked of us is for one purpose: that we might love him and love one another as Christ loves us!

Vertical Axis

The vertical axis represents our "direct" relationship with Jesus and the Father in the Holy Spirit.

Prayer

"Have no anxiety at all, but in everything, by prayer and petition, with thanksgiving, make your requests known to God. Then the peace of God that surpasses all understanding will guard your hearts and minds in Christ Jesus" (Philippians 4:6-7).

A relationship needs to have two directions: talking and listening. In prayer, we both talk and listen. In prayer we meet God and experience his love. As followers of Jesus, we pray communally as in our Eucharistic liturgy, but also privately, in our inner room, behind a closed door (Matthew 6:6) conversationally, paying attention as we would to a close friend. Our conversation with God is permeated with adoration, contrition, thanksgiving, and supplication.

Word

"Your word is a lamp for my feet and a light for my path" (Psalm 119:105).

God communicates his Word to us in many ways by primarily through the Scriptures and the Church. With the help of the Holy Spirit, when we read and meditate on his Word, we get to know him more and become closer to him. The teachings of the Church help guide us as we grow in this knowledge and assist us in living as Christ taught.

The Horizontal Axis

The horizontal axis represents our relationships with other people as members of Christ's body.

Community

"For where two or three are gathered together in my name, there am I in the midst of them" (Matthew 18:20).

The Holy Spirit binds us together in love. We need one another for support, encouragement, and accountability. Fostering relationships with others who have also made Christ the center of their life is key for growth and perseverance in following him. Being involved in a small Christian community, Bible study, or prayer group at your Church is a good way to do this.

Evangelization

"For I am not ashamed of the gospel. It is the power of God for the salvation of everyone who believes..." (Romans 1:16).

Evangelization is sharing the good news of Jesus Christ with people. We witness to the truth of the Gospel by how we live, what we say, and how we live in love with other believers (the witness of word, life, and community). The Church exists to bring the Gospel of Jesus Christ to the world. When we are following Jesus we want to share with others the joy, peace, and love we have found in him.

Appendix B

For Week 3: A Rich Sacramental Life

How did the Sacrament of Reconciliation Develop?

Excerpts from the Catechism of the Catholic Church:

1446 Christ instituted the Sacrament of Penance for all sinful members of his Church: above all for those who, since Baptism, have fallen into grave sin, and have thus lost their baptismal grace and wounded ecclesial communion. It is to them that the Sacrament of Penance offers a new possibility to convert and to recover the grace of justification. The Fathers of the Church present this sacrament as "the second plank [of salvation] after the shipwreck which is the loss of grace."[1]

1447 Over the centuries the concrete form in which the Church has exercised this power received from the Lord has varied considerably. During the first centuries the reconciliation of Christians who had committed particularly grave sins after their Baptism (for example, idolatry, murder, or adultery) was tied to a very rigorous discipline, according to which penitents had to do public penance for their sins, often for years, before receiving reconciliation. To this "order of penitents" (which concerned only certain grave sins), one was only rarely admitted and in certain regions only once in a lifetime. During the seventh century Irish missionaries, inspired by the Eastern monastic tradition, took to continental Europe the "private" practice of penance, which does not require public and prolonged completion of penitential works before reconciliation with the Church. From that time on, the sacrament has been performed in secret between penitent and priest. This new practice envisioned the possibility of repetition and so opened the way to a regular frequenting of this sacrament. It allowed the forgiveness of grave sins and venial sins to be integrated into one sacramental celebration. In its main lines this is the form of penance that the Church has practiced down to our day.

1448 Beneath the changes in discipline and celebration that this sacrament has undergone over the centuries, the same *fundamental structure* is to be discerned. It comprises two equally essential elements: on the one hand, the acts of the man who undergoes conversion through the action of the Holy Spirit: namely, contrition, confession, and satisfaction; on the other, God's action through the intervention of the Church. The Church, who through the bishop and his priests forgives sins in the name of Jesus Christ and determines the manner of satisfaction, also prays for the sinner and does penance with him. Thus the sinner is healed and re-established in ecclesial communion.

[1]Tertullian, De Paenit. 4, 2: PL 1, 1343; cf. Council of Trent (1547): DS 1542.

Appendix C

For Week 3: A Rich Sacramental Life

A Guide to the Sacrament of Reconciliation

If it has been a long time since you last "went to confession," you may be hesitant and unsure. Join the club! However, reconciling with God is always a cause of great joy in our lives. Take the plunge! You'll be glad you did. Below is a step-by-step description of the process that may help alleviate your fears. Keep in mind that you always have the option to go to confession privately behind a screen or face-to-face with the priest.

1. Prepare to receive the sacrament by praying and examining your conscience. Appendix D contains three versions of an examination of conscience for your use.

2. Begin by making the Sign of the Cross and greeting the priest by saying, "Bless me father, for I have sinned," and telling the priest how long it has been since your last confession.

3. Confess your sins to the priest. If you are unsure about some thing, ask him to help you. Place your trust in God, a merciful and loving father. When you are finished, indicate this by saying something like, "I am sorry for these and all of my sins."

4. The priest will assign you a penance such as prayer or a work of mercy, service or sacrifice.

5. Express sorrow for your sins by saying an act of contrition such as the one below.

6. The priest, acting in the person of Christ, will absolve you from your sins by saying the Prayer of Absolution, to which you respond by making the Sign of the Cross and saying, "Amen."

7. The priest will offer some proclamation of praise, such as "Give thanks to the Lord, for he is good," to which you respond, "His mercy endures forever."

8. The priest will dismiss you.

9. Go and complete your assigned penance.

An Act of Contrition

O my God, I am heartily sorry for having offended you and I detest all my sins, not only because I dread the loss of heaven and pains of hell, but most of all because they offend you, my God, who are all good and deserving of all my love. I firmly resolve, with the help of your grace, to confess my sins, to do penance, and to amend my life. Amen.

Appendix D

For Week 3: A Rich Sacramental Life

Examination of Conscience

Following are three examinations of conscience for young adults, single persons, and married persons from the United States Conference of Catholic Bishops website, written by Fr. Thomas Weinandy. Used with permission. For the introductions to these examinations by Fr. Weinandy, see the United States Conference of Catholic Bishop's website, www.usccb.org/lent/celebrate.shtml.

An Examination of Conscience for Young Adults

Responsibilities to God:

Have I gone to Mass on Sunday or have I rebelled and been stubborn about going to Mass? Did I participate in the Mass or did I daydream?

Have I prayed every day?

Have I read the Bible?

Have I been rebellious toward God and his commands?

Have I misused the name of God by swearing and cursing?

Have I told the Father that I love him for creating me and making me his son/daughter?

Have I thanked Jesus for becoming man, dying for my sin and rising to give me eternal life?

Have I asked the Holy Spirit to help me conquer sin and temptation and to be obedient to God's commands?

Responsibilities to others and myself:

Have I been rebellious, disobedient or disrespectful to my parents, teachers and those in authority over me?

Have I lied to or deceived my parents or others?

Have I been arrogant and stubborn?

Have I talked back to my parents or those in authority?

Have I gotten angry or nurtured and held grudges and resentments? Have I refused to forgive others? Have I cultivated hatred?

Have I engaged in sexual fantasies? Have I looked at others lustfully?

Have I read pornographic literature or looked at pornographic pictures, shows or movies?

Have I masturbated?

Have I lustfully kissed or sexually touched someone? Have I had sexual intercourse?

Have I had an abortion or encouraged another to have one?

Have I gossiped about others? Have I slandered anyone? Have I told lies about others? Have I mocked or made fun of others?

Have I lied or cheated?

Have I stolen anything? Have I paid it back?

Have I been selfish or spiteful toward others?

Have I been jealous?

Have I gotten drunk, or taken drugs?

Have I participated in anything that is of the occult: Ouija boards, fortune tellers, séances, channeling, astrology?

Have I been patient, kind, gentle and self-controlled?

When my conscience told me to do something good, did I do it or did I ignore it?

An Examination of Conscience for Single Persons

Responsibilities to God:

Have I gone to Mass every Sunday? Have I participated at Mass or have I daydreamed or been present with a blank mind?

Have I prayed every day (15-20 minutes)?

Have I read the Bible? Have I studied the truths of our faith and allowed them to become more a part of the way I think and act? Have I read any spiritual books or religious literature?

Have I told God that I want to love him with my whole heart, mind and strength? Do I hold any resentments toward God?

Have I recognized my need for Jesus and his salvation? Have I asked the Holy Spirit to empower me to live the Christian life?

Have I been financially generous to the Church? Have I participated in parish or religious activities?

Have I held resentments toward the Church or Church authorities? Have I forgiven them?

Responsibilities to others and to myself:

Have I been rebellious, disobedient or disrespectful to anyone in authority?

Have I lied to or deceived others—friends, boss, or coworkers?

Have I been arrogant and stubborn?

Have I gotten angry or nurtured and held grudges and resentments? Have I refused to forgive others—parents, relatives, employers, former friend, a former spouse? Have I cultivated hatred?

Have I felt sorry for myself or nurtured self-pity?

Have I engaged in sexual fantasies? Have I looked at others lustfully?

Have I read pornographic literature or looked at pornographic pictures, shows or movies?

Have I masturbated?

Have I lustfully kissed or sexually touched someone? Have I had sexual intercourse?

Have I had an abortion or encouraged another to have one?

Have I gossiped about others? Have I slandered anyone? Have I told lies about others? Have I mocked or made fun of others?

Responsibilities to society:

Have I been a Christian witness to those with whom I work or associate? Have I spoken to anyone about the Gospel and how important it is to believe in Jesus?

Have I allowed the Gospel to influence my political and social opinions?

Have I had a proper Christian concern for the poor and needy?

Have I paid my taxes?

Have I fostered or nurtured hatred toward my 'political' opponents, either local, national or international?

Have I been prejudiced toward others because of race, color, religion or social status?

An Examination of Conscience for Married Persons

Responsibilities to God:

Have I gone to Mass every Sunday? Have I participated at Mass or have I day dreamed or been present with a blank mind?

Have I prayed every day (15-20 minutes)?

Have I read the Bible? Have I studied the truths of our faith and allowed them to become more part of the way I think and act? Have I read any spiritual books or religious literature?

Have I told God that I want to love him with my whole heart, mind and strength? Do I hold any resentments toward God?

Have I recognized my need for Jesus and his salvation? Have I asked the Holy Spirit to empower me to live the Christian life, to be a proper husband/wife and parent?

Have I been financially generous to the Church? Have I participated in parish or religious activities?

Have I held resentments toward the Church or Church authorities? Have I forgiven them?

Responsibilities to my spouse:

Have I cared for my spouse? Have I been generous with my time? Have I been affectionate and loving? Have I told my spouse that I love him or her?

Have I been concerned about the spiritual well-being of my spouse?

Have I listened to my spouse? Have I paid attention to his or her concerns, worries, and problems? Have I sought these out?

Have I allowed resentments and bitterness toward my spouse to take root in my mind? Have I nurtured these? Have I forgiven my spouse for the wrongs he or she has committed against me?

Have I allowed misunderstanding, miscommunication or accidents to cause anger and mistrust? Have I nurtured critical and negative thoughts about my spouse?

Have I manipulated my spouse in order to get my own way?

Have I tried to bully or overpower my spouse?

Have I spoken sharply or sarcastically to my spouse? Have I spoken in a demeaning or negative way? Have I injured my spouse through taunting and negative teasing? Have I called my spouse harsh names or used language that is not respectful?

Have I physically abused my spouse?

Have I gossiped about my spouse?

Have I undermined the authority and dignity of my spouse through disrespect and rebelliousness?

Have I been moody and sullen?

Have I bickered with my spouse out of stubbornness and selfishness?

Have I lied or been deceitful to my spouse?

Have I misused sexuality? Have I used sexual relations solely for my own selfish pleasure? Have I been too demanding in my desire for sexual fulfillment? Have I been loving and physically affectionate in my sexual relations or have I used sexual relations in a way that would be demeaning or disrespectful to my spouse? Have I refused sexual relations out of laziness, revenge or manipulation?

Have I refused to conceive children out of selfishness or material greed? Have I used artificial means of contraception?

Have I had an abortion or encouraged others to have one?

Have I masturbated?

Have I flirted or fostered improper relationships with someone else, either in my mind or through words and actions?

Have I used pornography: books, magazines or movies?

Have I committed adultery?

Have I misused alcohol or drugs?

Have I been financially responsible?

Responsibilities to children:

Have I cared for the spiritual needs of my children? Have I been a shepherd and guardian as God has appointed me? Have I tried to foster a Christian family where Jesus is Lord? Have I taught my children the Gospel and the commandments of God?

Have I prayed with them?

Have I been persistent and courageous in my training and teaching? Have I disciplined them when necessary? Have I been lazy and apathetic?

Have I talked with them to find out their problems, concerns and fears? Have I been affectionate toward them? Have I hugged them and told them that I love them? Have I played or recreated with them?

Have I been impatient and frustrated with them? Have I corrected them out of love in order to teach them what is right and good? Have I treated them with respect? Have I spoken to them in a sarcastic or demeaning way?

Have I held resentments against them? Have I forgiven them?

Have I been of one heart and mind with my spouse in the upbringing of the children? Or have I allowed disagreements and dissension to disrupt the training, educating and disciplining of our children?

Have I undermined the role of authority in the eyes of my children by speaking negatively against God, the Church, my spouse or others who hold legitimate authority over them?

Have I been a good Christian witness to my children in what I say and do? Or do I demand one standard for them and another for myself?

Have I been properly generous with my children regarding money and physical and material well-being? Have I been miserly? Have I been extravagant, thus spoiling them?

Responsibilities to society:

Have I been a Christian witness to those with whom I work or associate? Have I spoken to anyone about the Gospel and how important it is to believe in Jesus?

Have I held resentments and anger against those with whom I work, relatives or friends? Have I forgiven them?

Have I been unethical in my business dealings? Have I stolen or lied?

Have I allowed the Gospel to influence my political and social opinions?

Have I had a proper Christian concern for the poor and needy?

Have I paid my taxes?

Have I fostered or nurtured hatred toward my "political" enemies, either local, national or international?

Have I been prejudiced toward others because of race, color, religion or social status?

Appendix E

For Week 5: Introduction to Praying with Scripture

Suggestions for Meditation

Books of the Bible in the New Testament to begin with:

Any of the 4 Gospels: *Matthew, Mark, Luke,* or *John*

Philippians

Colossians

1 Peter

Psalms

1 or 2 Corinthians

Website for printing out citations of daily readings for the liturgical year: http://www.usccb.org/nab/

Spiritual books to read for meditation:

Imitation of Christ by Thomas A'Kempis

He Cares for You by Corrie Ten-Boom

The Pursuit of God by A.W. Tozer

The Way, The Furrow, and The Forge by St. Josemaria Escriva

Word Among Us (publication with reflections on Sunday and daily readings)

Magnificat (publication with daily readings and meditations or reflections on theme of day by a Saint or theologian)

God and You by William Barry

Life and Holiness by Thomas Merton

Prayer is a Hunger by Farrell

Moment by Moment: A Retreat in Everyday Life by Carol Ann Smith and Eugene Merz. This is based on the spiritual exercises.

Appendix F

For Week 8: Evangelization

Comments on John 4: 3-43

From question 17: Trace what the characters wanted, what they ultimately received, and how they received it. Touch on the Samaritan woman, the disciples, the villagers and Jesus.

Samaritan Woman

- What she wanted: to be unseen; to get some water.

- What she ultimately received: recognition. Previously an outcast, she is included in salvation and socially in the village. She becomes a missionary, a fisher of men, a reaper of a rich harvest of souls.

- How she received it: Jesus approached her. She kept asking questions; she dared to argue (you say/we say). She risked leaving her water and bucket to tell her story (testimony).

The Disciples

- What they wanted: food; to meet their own and Jesus' needs; probably to stay clear of Samaritans.

- What they ultimately received: though their concern was with physical hunger and safety, they saw what happens when risks are taken, humans are recognized as such, and spiritual hunger is satisfied. They witnessed and possibly participated in the reaping.

- How they received it: They stay with Jesus, even in a dangerous land. They followed where Jesus led, watched what he did, and probably ultimately participated as they were able.

The Villagers

- What they wanted: They wanted Jesus to stay with them; they want a messiah.

- What they ultimately received: the presence of Jesus among them; direct knowledge of him.

- How they received it: They listened to the testimony of another, were intrigued, and then investigated for themselves.

<u>Jesus</u>

- What he wanted: water, he was thirsty, maybe some rest, possibly a foothold for God among the Samaritans.

- What he ultimately received: an opportunity to give spiritually to a woman isolated and in need, and through her to meet a whole village.

- How he received it: he took the opportunity to talk despite fatigue and thirst, broke custom by talking with a Samaritan and a woman. His deep relationship with God provided inside knowledge of her circumstances. He took her questions seriously but answered the real question instead of the superficial ones.

the evangelical Catholic
forming disciples. training leaders.

www.evangelicalcatholic.org

Made in the USA
Lexington, KY
23 January 2018